Wild Ride

Wild Ride

*My Journey from Cancer Kid
to Astronaut*

Adapted for Young Readers

Hayley Arceneaux

WITH SANDRA BARK

CONVERGENT
New York

Published in the United States by Convergent Books,
an imprint of Random House, a division of
Penguin Random House LLC, New York.

CONVERGENT BOOKS is a registered trademark and the Convergent
colophon is a trademark of Penguin Random House LLC.

Adapted from the adult version of *Wild Ride* by Hayley Arceneaux,
published in hardcover by Convergent Books, an imprint of
Random House, a division of Penguin Random House LLC,
in 2022. Copyright © 2022 by Hayley Arceneaux.

LIBRARY OF CONGRESS CATALOGING-IN-PUBLICATION DATA
Names: Arceneaux, Hayley, author. | Bark, Sandra, author.
Title: Wild ride: (adapted for young readers) / by Hayley Arceneaux;
with Sandra Bark.
Other titles: Wild ride (Young reader's adaptation)
Description: New York: Convergent Books, [2023] |
Audience: Ages 8-12 | Audience: Grades 4-6
Identifiers: LCCN 2023011961 (print) | LCCN 2023011962 (ebook) |
ISBN 9780593443880 (Hardback; acid-free paper) |
ISBN 9780593443897 (Ebook)
Subjects: LCSH: Arceneaux, Hayley | Women astronauts—United
States—Biography—Juvenile literature. | Physicians' assistants—
United States—Biography—Juvenile literature. | Cancer—
Patients—United States—Biography—Juvenile literature. | Space
medicine—United States—Juvenile literature. | Space flight—
Juvenile literature.
Classification: LCC TL789.85.A73 A3 2023 (print) |
LCC TL789.85.A73 (ebook) |
DDC 629.450092 [B]—dc23/eng/20230322
LC record available at https://lccn.loc.gov/2023011961
LC ebook record available at https://lccn.loc.gov/2023011962

Printed in Canada on acid-free paper

crownpublishing.com

2 4 6 8 9 7 5 3 1

First Edition

Book design by Alexis Capitini

To Mom, Dad, and Hayden,
by my side, through it all

Contents

Part 2: Dreams

Introduction

Hello, Fellow Traveler!

Thank you for joining me on this journey. Over the course of this book, you're going to get to know me very well. Which has me wondering about you! As I write these words, I am trying to imagine you, the person who will be going on this adventure with me. There's so much I don't know about you. I don't know how old you are, or what country you live in, or where you go to school, your favorite food, or even if you have pets.

Here is where I have landed: I think you are someone who is very curious. I think you are someone who wants to take on the world and make it your own. Someone who looks up at the stars at night and wonders what all is out there. In short—someone just like me!

Am I right? Am I close?

I think I must be. I mean, aren't we all curious about the world around us? Aren't we all wondering what amazing things might happen in our lives? I know I am. I've been around the world, I've been to space, and I'm still dreaming of the new, incredible experiences I might get to have someday. There are just so many different places to explore, new things to try to learn, and people to talk to. Talking to people is one of my very favorite things to do. People are kind and funny, and you can learn a lot from someone else's story, if they are willing to tell it to you, and if you are willing to take the time to listen.

That's why I wrote this book—to share my experience with you. This is my story of being a sick kid. It's my story of being brave despite feeling scared and hoping that I could get better so that I could live life to the fullest. And it's my story about going to outer space.

I wrote it so that people who have never had cancer could learn something about what it is to get sick and then get better again. So that kids who go through tough times will know how important it is to hold on to hope, and that hope can carry you forward. So that people who dream about going to outer space, who have looked at the stars and thought, *I wonder . . . ,* could get a feeling for what that might be like and know that it is possible.

When you read a story, it becomes a part of you. When you read this book, I hope that you get the feeling that anything is possible. That if you are sick, you can get well again. That if you are scared, you can find your inner bravery and your own strength.

So high five to you. To the kids who go to school even though there are bullies. To the kids whose mom or dad isn't around anymore. To the kids who try their hardest, do their best, and hold on to hope.

Life has so many ups and downs. The more you believe in the ups, the more you can get through the downs.

So let's get on with it. I've just heard from mission control that the rocket is about to launch. Do you have everything you need for the journey before we take off, fellow traveler? Do you have a snack, a drink, your favorite sweatshirt? Take your seat and get comfortable. And don't forget to buckle up.

It's going to be a wild ride.

Part 1

Hopes

So much to do, so much to see.
—Smash Mouth, "All Star"

CHAPTER 1

How to Pack for Outer Space

Once upon a time, there was a girl who rode a Dragon to the stars . . .

It's a quiet evening in Memphis, and I'm getting ready for the trip of a lifetime.

"Scarlett," I say, "in two weeks, I'm going to space."

My beautiful, fluffy, gray Aussiedoodle looks up at me with an expression of love and mild concern on her face. She's not worried about me. She's wondering who will watch her when I'm gone.

"The boys are going to take amazing care of you," I tell my dog, knowing she'll be safe and happy with our favorite neighbors.

Her expression relaxes, and I continue. She's heard it all since the beginning of this wild year: the Dragon spacecraft, the Falcon 9 rocket, the fact that we're going deeper into space than anyone has been in over twenty years.

I can't wait. There's nothing I love more than traveling to a place I've never been before.

Plus, I hear the views are incredible.

In case you're wondering, no, this is not the beginning of a sci-fi fairy tale.

Forget science fiction. This is science fact, and the fact is that very soon I'll be strapping into a spacecraft with my crew. Our mission: After launch, we'll be 370 miles above the surface of Earth, orbiting for three days at 17,500 miles an hour before we splash back down in the Atlantic Ocean. For reference, the International Space Station hangs out 250 miles up.

Packing for an adventure is something I do pretty often. I've packed for trips to Spanish beaches (bathing suit, sunscreen, book, hat) and I've packed for camel-riding trips in the Sahara Desert in Morocco (long-sleeved shirt, tall boots, headscarf). Deciding what to bring to outer space is nothing like that.

Luckily, most of what I need will be supplied by the mission. Just a week after I was selected, I was fitted for a sharp white space suit by a woman who used to make superhero costumes for movies. That was nine months ago. Now launch is only days away. I'm no superhero and this isn't a movie, but . . . let's just say I can't wait to wear that space suit.

———

I will never forget the day I got The Call.

It was January 5, 2021, nine months before I started packing for space, and I had a call with St. Jude.

St. Jude, more formally known as St. Jude Children's Research Hospital, is an amazing place for kids who have cancer. It's where I work as a physician assistant or, as we call it, a PA. It's the same place that treated *me* for bone cancer when I was a kid. Since then, I've done a lot of fundraising for them, traveling around and telling people about the hospital so that other kids can have the same kind of care I had.

It wasn't unusual to have a call scheduled, but there was something about this call that felt different. I always trust my gut. In that moment, my gut was twisted up like a bowl of spaghetti. Something was coming. I could feel it.

I called in.

"Hayley, we want to talk to you about something really big," they said.

They told me about a billionaire named Jared Isaacman who was leading the first all-civilian mission to space. By "all-civilian" they meant that no NASA or other professional astronauts would be on board. The best part was that it was going to be a fundraising mission for St. Jude.

What did this have to do with me, I started to wonder. I didn't have to wonder for long.

"We'd love to send you."

"Me?" I laughed. It was the only natural response. "Are you serious?"

They were. They were very serious. Four people would be going to space. Did I want to go?

In that moment I realized that I did. I really wanted to go.

"Will you consider it?"

"Yes!"

After that, it was like talking about any other trip, except that I felt like I was in a dream. "Space, wow! For how long?"

"Three days."

"Let me talk to my family," I said. "But my answer is yes."

I got off the phone and looked down at my hands and saw they were shaking. My whole body was shaking.

I FaceTimed Mom.

"You are not going to believe this," I said to her.

I wasn't sure what she would say. My family has been through a lot with me. I had bone cancer when I was ten. I had three surgeries on my leg between the ages of ten and fifteen. There were points where I thought, *Am I ever going to be off crutches? Am I ever going to be able to walk?* My family went through all of that with me.

And now I was calling to say that . . .

"I just got invited to go to space."

"WHAT?"

"It's true," I said.

Mom's eyes were bright; she looked so excited for me.

"Mom, I can't pass up this opportunity," I continued.

"No, you can't," she said. "This is once in a lifetime."

We looked at each other and she said, "Call Hayden."

That's what Mom always says. Any issue, her response is "Call your brother." Hayden is the logical one in the family. He's the one in our family who loves space—so much that he actually became a real-life rocket scientist.

Hayden answered his cellphone from his desk at work, where he is an aerospace engineer.

"It's not an emergency," I said quickly. My family has seen enough of those to share news and information in a way that doesn't scare the other person to pieces.

"I have to talk to you right now. You need to go outside."

I waited until he was ready and then said, "Hayden, I got invited to go to space." I watched the shock come over his face while my mom, who was also on the Face-Time, smiled like crazy. I hadn't asked enough questions on the call with St. Jude, I was realizing. "Do you think going to space is safe?" I asked him.

"Well, nothing is a hundred percent, but I think it's safe," he told me.

I emailed St. Jude that night to tell them YES I would go to space! I also asked more questions. "Are we going to any destinations, like the International Space Station? Are we going to the moon?"

When I told my brother about my questions, he rolled his eyes. "Hayley, that was so dumb. You asked if you were going to the moon?"

"Why is that dumb?"

"We haven't been to the moon in decades."

"How was I supposed to know that?"

Well, now I know: The moon is 238,900 miles away.

These days, I know a lot more than I did when I first got The Call. For instance, once we strap into our seats and launch, it will take less than ten minutes to get to space. Those ten minutes are going to be physically uncomfortable, with G-forces pressing us down into our seats. But that's what I've been training for. As Jared, our commander, said early on, we needed to get comfortable with discomfort. And boy, did we.

Over the past nine months, I've been spun around and turned upside down, climbed a mountain, and even practiced swimming in a motorcycle helmet. None of it was easy. The hardest part was wishing I could share it with my dad. He passed away four years ago, and I still forget that I can't just call him. It will be left-handed appreciation day, and he is left-handed, and I'm about to call him to say, "Happy left-hander's day!" when I remember that he's gone.

I wish I could tell him that I am going to space. He would have loved hearing it so much. I never got to tell him that I got the job at St. Jude, but he could have predicted that. That was in the stars for me. But space? He never would have guessed this. None of us could have guessed.

Instead, I packed something very special, just for him, one of our inside jokes: his tie. It was his favorite.

The tie is covered with drawings of faces of kids and flags. I mean, it's ugly. It's a very ugly tie. It's also a St. Jude tie.

I would always say, "Dad, don't wear that tie."

And he would say, "No, I'm gonna wear it. Because then people will ask me about it, and I get to tell them about St. Jude."

We had that conversation about a million times.

Now it's the perfect thing to bring to space to honor him. It gives me goosebumps.

I know he'd be so proud of me, and that once we reach zero gravity, all of my hard work will be worth it. I'm going to take out Dad's tie, float around in our capsule, eat M&M's like Ms. Pac-Man, and have a long,

long look at this planet, the place where I have lived my entire beautiful, mysterious, incredible life so far.

It may be hard to believe while I'm gravity-bound on my bedroom floor, but if there's one thing I've learned in my time on Earth, it's that as long as you keep saying yes, everything is possible.

CHAPTER 2

Purple Tongues and Black Belts

When I was seven, I was famous on my street in St. Francisville, Louisiana, for my dog, Chloe, who had a purple tongue.

Chloe held a place of honor in my family too. Before I was born, before my little brother, Hayden, before my dad was even in the picture, it had been my mom and Chloe. And Chloe was the reason my parents met in the first place.

I loved when they told the story of how they met.

Mom would say, "Well, there was an older guy who lived across the street."

Dad would jump in with "I would notice this pretty girl now and again."

I can picture it in my mind. Mom, a PhD student in her twenties, with long brown hair and the cutest little puppy in the world. Dad, a journalist with a large moustache, which I am told was very stylish for the time.

Mom: "I was taking my new puppy, Chloe, out for a walk."

Dad: "It was the perfect opportunity to meet my neighbor."

Mom: "He walked up to me, and Chloe got so excited."

Dad: "So excited that she peed on my foot."

Mom: "My first words to Dad were 'Oh my gosh, did my dog just pee on you?'"

Dad: "I said, 'No.'"

Mom: "Then he wiped his shoe on the grass."

That's why I'm here today. Because a small dog with a purple tongue couldn't hold it in.

That was the beginning of my family.

I was in second grade when my dad, who loved martial arts movies, first suggested that we take tae kwon do together.

"Yes!" I said.

Anything he suggested, I wanted to do, because I really wanted to be like my dad. Hayden, my little brother, also wanted to go. Mom volunteered to be our audience.

Tae kwon do classes were held at a local studio in our hometown twice a week. It was the same studio where I was already taking dance and gymnastics. The studio was one-size-fits-all, basically a large room with white walls and mats in the center on the floor, with ballet barres and mirrors and a balance beam, vault, and gymnastics bars in the corner.

As much as I liked dance and gymnastics, I knew right away that tae kwon do was destined to be my true love.

In our first class, they explained how it would work. We would be learning forms, which were sequences of punches, blocks, and kicks. We would begin with a white belt, then move up through a rainbow of colors until we reached black. Each color belt had a different form. Once you mastered the forms, along with breaking boards and sparring with a partner, you could move on to the next color.

"I'm going all the way to black belt," I told Dad after our first class.

He nodded. He was in.

It was on.

From that very first class, I was obsessed. I always wanted to be well prepared, so I spent a lot of time practicing my forms in our living room at home. Before class, I would change into my white uniform, tying the belt with special care, dreaming of the day when my white belt would be replaced by the black belt. On the weekends, my friends and I would go to the local video store and rent martial arts movies to watch during our sleepovers. The thrill I got when the nunchucks went whooshing through the air!

Hayden lost interest in tae kwon do after a few sessions. His head was in space; he kept asking to go to NASA, and we planned a trip. Dad and I stayed with tae kwon do. Over the next couple of months, we went from white belt to yellow belt pretty fast.

In order to get the next belt, we had to break a board in half. I loved breaking boards. There's such a rush that comes from putting all your strength and aim into a move and then feeling that thick piece of wood split in two. I would scream a powerful "HUH!" every time I broke a board. It gave me an extra boost of force.

I was still keeping up with my dance classes, which meant that at our recitals, I was also a part of the tae kwon do group who put on the intermission performance as the dancers changed costumes. I had no break at all during dance performances. With my face full of makeup from dance, I would run and quickly put on my tae kwon do uniform for the intermission performance, then change again into my next tutu for act 2.

It was a hectic schedule, but I didn't care. It was worth it.

Level by level, Dad and I moved up the ranks. Gold and orange, then green, blue, purple, red, red with a stripe . . .

That summer, the summer I was nine and Hayden was six, we took a family trip to NASA. We toured the facility, saw moon rocks, and ate ice cream that came in little pellets, the same kind astronauts eat in space (or so we thought). Hayden was so excited we were there. He kept running from exhibit to exhibit, learning details and then coming back to share them with us. Mom and Dad and Hayden and I had our picture taken in front of a green screen. In the photo, we are floating together as a family in zero gravity. Of course, we weren't really floating; one of the employees edited the photo to make it look that way.

That trip to visit NASA was the highlight of Hayden's summer. To me, it was a fun trip, but I was more focused on getting ready for my brown-belt test. It was coming soon, and I wanted to be ready.

Before I knew it, it was the day for my brown-belt test.

Before my turn, Dad and I stood on the sidelines, talking quietly.

"I don't know if I can do it," I told him. I had practiced so much, but I wasn't sure I was ready.

"You can do it," Dad assured me.

When it was my turn, I took a deep breath, straightened my shoulders, and stepped forward. I made my "HUH!" even louder than usual, pushing myself to be strong. And it worked! The board cracked under my hands. I left that day with my brown belt. And something even more important: a feeling of confidence. Dad was proud of me too. He saved a piece of the board I'd broken that day and used it to write me a message.

"I'm more proud of you for conquering your fear than for earning your brown belt," it read.

I was in fourth grade by the time we got to our black-belt test day. It had taken two and a half years to get to this point, and Dad and I were both ready. But this time, I was more unsure than ever.

Mom was in the crowd with Hayden, filming and taking pictures, giving the occasional wave as I went through the different parts of the test: sparring with other students, breaking boards with both my fists and my feet, and doing my form.

The problem was, I got so nervous that midway through my form, I went blank. I forgot the moves.

After the test, they gathered us at the front of the room to give out the belts.

Dad passed. I did not. I had failed, utterly failed. Dad was finally a black belt. I was stuck at brown.

This was not okay with me. I was used to being good at things. I aced things with ease. I was an all-A student and always made honor roll—when I got my first B at school, it just made me want to try harder. I liked being the best I could be, and I liked the feeling of accomplishment from working hard and succeeding.

This was by far the biggest disappointment, the most crushing defeat, I had ever known. But I knew I wasn't going to give up.

I was going to get that black belt no matter what.

It was around this time that my leg started to hurt.

"Look at my knees," I would say.

It was just a coincidence that my dad had been complaining about exactly the same thing. Soon after he got his black belt, he had surgery on his knee.

"My knee hurts!" he would say again and again, staring at his legs.

He would put his knees together for comparison, to show that one was more swollen than the other, and I would look at them and try to see what he was showing me. "My knee hurts" and "Look at my knees" became common Dad phrases in our household.

I'd tell my family that my knee hurt too, but unlike Dad's swollen knee, my knees were the same size.

"My knee hurts," Dad would say.

"My knee hurts too," I would say.

I complained for a few weeks, pointing at my left knee again and again.

Mom took me to the doctor, but he couldn't see anything wrong. No injury was visible, which was not a relief to the doctor.

"I'd feel better if I saw an injury," he said. What he

did notice was that my left knee was warmer than the right.

He recommended pain medicines and to stay off the leg for a while. Not easy when you're training for your black belt, you know what I mean? I rested, as I was told, although it wasn't easy. With the help of the meds, I felt a little better, continued my training, and scheduled another black-belt test.

My second black-belt test came around, and I was nervous. Really nervous. I stood on the sidelines, gathering all my courage, thinking of Dad telling me I could do it. Instead of focusing on what had happened the last time I took my black-belt test, I thought about getting my brown belt. I had been scared. But I had found my strength and I had done the forms perfectly and had even broken that board.

I looked out and saw Mom with her camera, smiling in my direction, encouraging me. I saw Dad sitting next to her, willing me to do my best. Hayden was beside them, ready to cheer me on.

I sparred with as much focus and concentration as I could. Then it came time to do the forms.

Huh! HUH!

This time, I did it. I did it! I finally earned my black belt!

At home afterward, we had a big celebration. There

was even a cake decorated with a picture of a black belt with "Congratulations!" written below it.

What I remember from that day is just feeling so happy and so excited for whatever would come next, like I could do anything I wanted to do. Getting my black belt had changed me. It had made me stronger. It taught me my own power.

There was so much I didn't know in that moment. I had no way of knowing that this would be my last day ever practicing tae kwon do, or that all that strength I had built up would be serving me in a different way.

I also didn't know how soon I would need to rely on that strength.

CHAPTER 3

A Strange Lump

Every morning at the early hour of 7:45 A.M., I would ride with Mom to school. She was our school psychologist, and her office was near my classroom, so Hayden and I got rides every day.

It was a Monday after school, and I was lagging behind Mom and Hayden in the parking lot.

Mom looked my way. "Come on, Hayley," she said.

I tried to move faster, but my knee was hurting. It had ached and throbbed all day, no matter how hard I tried to ignore it.

"Hayley," called Mom again, "can you hurry up?"

"My knee hurts, Mom," I said.

Mom turned around and watched me walk toward her. "Are you limping?" she said. "You are. Are you okay? I'll look at it when we get home."

"It just hurts."

I climbed into the car beside Hayden and we headed home.

Mom was making pancakes, my favorite after-school treat. I limped into the kitchen, and she turned to stare at me midflip.

"Let me look at you," she said.

It was the first warm day in late January, and to celebrate, I had worn shorts. She knelt down to look at my knee and gasped, then stood and turned off the burner. Pancakes were forgotten.

"How long have you had this?"

"What?"

She pointed. Clearly visible beneath the bottom of my shorts was an egg-sized lump, just above my knee.

"I don't know," I said. "I don't usually look at my legs."

Mom grabbed the phone from the wall and the phone book and called my pediatrician. It was the end of the day, and the doctor was leaving, but she was promised the first appointment in the morning. Mom looked worried.

We still needed our afternoon snack. Mom turned the burner back on and finished making the pancakes.

That day, the pancakes didn't taste as good as they usually did.

———

At 7:00 A.M. the next morning I went to the pediatrician with both of my parents. My dad and I were light-hearted, making jokes. I was hoping to get a wrap bandage out of it, because it would have been so cool to get to wear it to school. But Mom was not laughing.

The pediatrician assessed the lump above my knee and said it felt bony.

"Let's get an X-ray," she said.

After the X-ray, the tech gave me a lollipop. From where I was sitting, all in all, it was a good morning, even though I still didn't have a cool bandage.

We waited in the exam room for what felt like ages before she came back in. "This is what I was suspecting," she said. "Osteosarcoma. Bone cancer."

I didn't know the word "osteosarcoma," but I knew the word "cancer." What I didn't understand yet was that you could have cancer and get better.

My parents were crying.

I burst into tears.

That moment was the most scared I've ever felt.

I walked out of the doctor's office, crying and holding my dad. I saw other kids in the waiting room looking at me and thought they might think I was a wimp who was crying over getting a shot or something. I wanted to tell them that this was not the case! But saying that I had cancer didn't feel right either.

What I was worrying about wasn't just the idea of cancer. What about *school*?

"I have to go back," I told my parents. "I have perfect attendance!"

I returned to school and told my teachers and classmates what was happening. My teachers looked confused and concerned. I didn't mind the extra attention they gave me.

It turned out to be my last day of school for nearly a year.

I knew I would miss seeing my friends and teachers every day. I would miss just how normal it felt to wake up early and go to class and do homework in the evenings. I would miss feeling like a regular ten-year-old.

While I was at school, my dad was researching my type of cancer online. When he found the website for St. Jude, he called and asked if they would take me. A few days later, my mom sat down with me in the study and told me that I needed to pack.

"We're going to a cancer hospital in Memphis, Tennessee, for a few weeks or so," she said while we both cried. My fourth-grade class was studying state geography, and I had learned where Tennessee was. It felt very far away.

Before we left, I sat with Dad and we looked through a catalog of wigs. I knew that people with cancer went bald because of their medications, and I was terrified at the thought of the same thing happening to me. Dad assured me that we could find a wig that would look natural when the time came, and that helped me feel better.

It was a Monday when I started limping. Tuesday, I was diagnosed with cancer. By Friday, we were on our way to Memphis. My dad left first, driving so we would have a car. Mom and I flew to "the cancer hospital." Hayden was staying with our grandparents.

I had flown on a plane a few times before, and now I sat next to Mom, drinking apple juice from a plastic cup, looking out the window at the views of farmland below us.

I was calm until we landed in Memphis, and then I freaked out.

"I hate Memphis," I said to Mom while we were carrying our suitcases to the shuttle bus. "It's horrible here. Why would anyone live here?"

I was so scared. I didn't know how to say that, so I got angry at Memphis instead.

All I wanted was someone to tell me that I was going to be okay.

We walked in the doors of St. Jude for the very first time, Mom and I together.

Mom walked up to the front desk, holding my MRI films.

"I'm here with my daughter, Hay—"

She started to say my name but instead burst into tears. The receptionist came around the front desk and gave her a big hug.

"Don't worry. It's going to be okay. You're part of the St. Jude family now," Ms. Penny said to Mom. "We'll take care of her, and we'll take care of you too."

CHAPTER 4

The New Normal

My first cancer accessory was a set of bright-red crutches, even better than the wrap bandage I had been imagining. My new medical team didn't want me to stand on my leg because I could break my thigh bone, thanks to the tumor.

I had no experience with crutches—I'd never broken a bone or even sprained an ankle before.

The nurse who was escorting me smiled her encouragement.

"You can do it," she said, smiling big at me as I swung on these new, shiny, cherry-red things. She had long blond hair, and she said she would be going with me to all of my appointments. There were so many things to do. She told me that she would explain each of them to me.

I was grateful to have this nurse at my side, helping us learn the ropes, making me laugh, and making the first day a little less scary. After each appointment I got to choose a prize from the prize box. My favorite was a tube of red lipstick, which I immediately started wearing.

Red lips, red crutches, I was ready for whatever might come my way.

St. Jude put my family up in a hotel a few blocks away from the hospital, where we would be staying until we could get into their housing facility.

On day one, I discovered the joy of the hotel's glass elevators, which went up nineteen stories. While my parents were settling in, I took my new crutches for a spin down the hallway, stopped in front of the elevator bank, and pressed the up arrow. The doors slid open and I got in. I pressed 19 and rode to the top, watching the world open up in front of me. Once I had soaked it all in, I pushed *L* for lobby. The elevator headed down. I stayed on, pressed the button for the top floor, and did it all over again. Other people got on and off while I just kept enjoying the ride and the views of the skyline. Maybe Memphis wasn't so bad after all.

My parents and I were sharing the hotel room. Dad kept trying to lighten the mood. Mom, who usually had a sense of humor, had her serious face on. I was focused on mastering the crutches, and it didn't take me long to get the hang of it. Soon I was swinging on them.

"Look!" I said.

I called them to the door to watch, then took off down the hallway, as fast as I could go. I was thrilled at my skill, having discovered that I could go faster on crutches than I could on foot, especially with my knee aching. After days of limping, it was nice having these pieces of plastic to speed me up.

Mom was less thrilled, and her voice carried a warning. "Slow down," she said.

I looked to Dad to tell her to stop worrying, but he had a worried face too.

It made me so angry. I spun around, threw down the crutches, and stomped on my bad leg. Usually I was a good kid, but there were so many changes going on. It was all too much.

"Hayley!" they both said.

Nobody was laughing. Dad looked really upset. If I was trying to get a rise out of them, it had worked. My rebellion didn't last long: A second later I felt guilty at having stressed them out; they were stressed enough already.

I picked the crutches back up and promised to use them at a more reasonable pace.

In the coming days, I would become more familiar with the hospital and with all the big words getting thrown at me. "Osteosarcoma," it turned out, was a fancy word for my kind of bone cancer.

It helped when I met with the child life specialist, who was there to help me understand what was going on.

To help explain it, she gave me a baby doll.

The first surgery I needed would insert a central line, a thin tube called a catheter, that would go into my chest and into a deep vein. It would be used to give me medication and to draw my blood.

We leaned over the doll, and I touched the smooth space on her chest where the catheter would go. Then she helped me carefully insert the central line into the doll's body, just like a surgeon. We added stitches, just like the ones I would be getting a few days later.

I slept with that doll every night.

Biopsy day. I was told the doctors would remove a small piece of my tumor and look at it under the microscope to confirm it was cancer. If I woke up from my surgery with the central line in my chest, I would know that I had cancer. If there was no line, then the lump wasn't cancer. But the chance of its not being cancer was slim.

My mom walked me back to the operating room, covered head to toe in medical gear: a sterile bunny suit, gloves, hairnet, and shoe covers. She was by my side as they were about to put me to sleep.

She leaned over and asked, "Is there anything you want? A special gift after this surgery?"

I didn't even hesitate before replying, "An Expedition car."

She rolled her eyes.

"Okay, you can put her to sleep now," Mom joked to the doctor.

I woke up from surgery feeling groggy and touched my chest. My fingers met a new bulge in the center where my central line had been placed.

"I have cancer?" I asked. I knew the answer, but I wanted confirmation.

Someone said, "Yes."

"Aww, man," I said, and fell headfirst into an unexpected future.

To cheer me up, my mom promised me a special gift. Instead of a car—I was only ten, after all—I could have something even better to look forward to when I was finished with treatment: a puppy.

Until then, my new schedule was chemotherapy aka chemo (medicine they would give me to help treat my cancer), blood tests, and more chemo. The treatments hit me hard. I would throw up, nearly nonstop, for days. In the weeks that followed, I could barely eat and I felt weak.

"You must be the most sensitive-stomached patient I've ever had," my doctor said.

I distracted myself with dog TV shows and books

with pictures of dogs. In between bouts of throwing up, I would get back into bed, pull a book onto my lap, and lose myself in dreams of the fun I would have with my dog, just as soon as I finished treatment.

Another ray of sunshine for me was my nurse Lizzie. I was an inpatient (staying in the hospital) every couple of weeks for chemo and whenever I had surprise problems like fevers. I always hoped Lizzie would be my nurse when I was in the hospital. As luck would have it, she usually was. Like me, Lizzie came from a small town in the South and was as sweet as pie. She was someone who could throw my sass back at me. I loved her.

During my sickest days in the hospital, Lizzie helped clean up more than her fair share of vomit. She made those hospital stays a great deal happier.

I was so impressed by my doctors and nurses, and I decided that I wanted to do what they did. When I grew up, I was going to help kids going through cancer treatment get better. I told everyone there that someday I would come back to work with them.

Since I couldn't go home much during treatment, we all fell into a routine. Dad and Hayden were in my hometown all week, Dad working and Hayden in school, while Mom and I were in Memphis. I missed them, and I missed my dog, Chloe, and I missed my friends back home in Louisiana a lot.

Mom and I were getting used to living together in the apartment in St. Jude housing. Even though our apartment had two bedrooms, when I wasn't in the hospital, I often slept in Mom's room because I didn't want to be alone.

Every weekend, Dad and Hayden would drive up to visit. I would be sitting in front of the window of our apartment, waiting for them to arrive for what always felt like hours. Finally, I would see my dad's black car pull up. Then I would rush to grab the scooter my parents had given me, which was by the door, and zoom down the hallway to meet them. Turns out you really need only one good leg to go fast.

I was staying up to date on what my class was learning back home with the help of a teacher through the St. Jude school. We practiced multiplication and division together. She would give me homework assignments, but usually the next time I saw her I would tell her I hadn't felt well enough to do my homework. (Maybe that wasn't always 100 percent true.)

What was hard was knowing that other people were out in the world having fun while I wasn't. Hayden got to see *Beauty and the Beast* in the theater while I was stuck in the hospital being sick. That one really hurt.

At first, I felt jealous. Then I felt sorry for myself.

After that, my family tried not to let me know when Hayden was doing fun things while I couldn't.

When I found out that Hayden had gone to a water park with our cousin Lauren, it was too much for me, and I complained to my mom.

"It's just not fair!"

Someone on the medical team, who was known for being a little rougher around the edges, happened to be in the room. She turned to me and said, "Well, life's not fair, kid, especially when you've got cancer."

My mom and I looked at each other, stunned. She left the room, and we burst out laughing at how she wasn't even trying to sugarcoat things for me! On another level, I knew that what she was saying was true.

One of the most difficult parts of going through cancer treatment? Losing my hair, which was a side effect from the chemo. I had known that it was coming ever since I had gotten the cancer diagnosis.

It started with strands of hair on my pillowcase. I would get so upset seeing them. It made my cancer seem even more real.

"I think it's time to get your hair cut short," Mom said one day. "It will be easier."

"Okay," I said.

So she found a salon nearby.

When we got there, the stylist sat me in her chair,

gently let my hair fall, and then said, "I think if we cut it just under your ears, it will be adorable." I had never had short hair before and I loved it.

The new short haircut worked for a while, but whenever I brushed or even touched my hair, more would fall out. Mom was constantly cleaning behind me so that I wouldn't realize how much I was losing.

I was at home in St. Francisville for a short visit in between chemo treatments when my hair started falling out in larger clumps. There in my bedroom, I realized that I couldn't take it anymore. My mom came into the room and sat down next to me as I put my hand up to my head. I pulled at the ends of some of the strands. I knew what would happen, and it did—the hair came out easily, wrapped around my fingers. I pulled on a larger clump, and then another. Handful by handful I pulled all of my hair out. I cried while I did it, though it didn't hurt.

When I looked in the mirror, I didn't know the girl who was looking back at me.

My mom tried to comfort me.

"You look beautiful," she told me. "You are beautiful."

I didn't believe her. I closed my eyes so I didn't have to see my bald head in the mirror. Without my hair, I barely recognized myself.

In the weeks I was losing my hair, I had been worried that my dog, Chloe, wouldn't recognize me. I didn't need to worry, though, because even though I was bald Chloe ran into my arms, just like she always did.

With or without my hair, I was still me.

At St. Jude, there were a lot of other kids who understood what I was going through, and I got to meet so many new friends. I met Hannah and Katie early on in my treatment. Those two were always up for playing pranks on the staff.

When we were in the hospital getting treatment, we would be attached to I.V. poles that held bags full of fluids and medication. The poles were on wheels, so you could take them with you when you were on the go. I could always count on entertainment from Hannah, who once put a goldfish in her I.V. bag and casually walked by the nurses' station. I could not stop laughing.

"You troublemakers!" the nurses would say, trying not to laugh themselves when they would catch on.

I, the inherent rule follower, protested.

"I'm not!" I said.

Of course, they didn't believe me.

Katie had a wild streak too, like the time she got out her Silly String and sprayed the child life specialists with colorful, slimy string. (We had no idea then that Katie would grow up to become a child life specialist herself.)

Right at the beginning, we asked one another questions to see how much we had in common. Turned out that we all had bone cancer and were around the same age. We all had to have chemotherapy and surgery. We also loved Harry Potter.

With them by my side, I found my place in this strange new world.

CHAPTER 5

Dr. Doom and the Cutting-Edge Prosthesis

When I first went to the hospital, my understanding of the human body was your basic head, shoulders, knees, and toes. But it didn't take long before I felt like an expert on the human leg.

My first anatomy teacher was my surgeon, Dr. Neel. In order to treat my bone cancer and save my leg, he was going to replace the cancer bone with an internal prosthesis, which was basically a new bone made of metal. This prosthesis was cutting-edge technology because even though it was metal, it could grow, whenever it was time for me to grow, without needing more surgeries to make it longer. That was a very big deal, because a leg surgery like this takes a long time to heal from. We're talking years, not months.

Dr. Neel, whom I quickly started calling Dr. Doom,

was a very good doctor. Dr. Doom wasn't like most adults. He didn't treat me like a baby and pretend it was all going to be easy. He just told it straight and honestly. It was scary at times, but it was something I appreciated.

Before the surgery, he drew my bone with the tumor and his plan for surgery on the paper covering the exam table.

"Remember, I went to medical school, not art school," he said.

That was obvious!

Then I went to see the child life specialist, where we operated on my doll again. This time the surgery involved a silver bendy straw that we put into the doll's leg so that I could learn about my growable prosthesis.

The weekend before my big surgery, Mom and I drove home to Louisiana so I could see my friends and family.

I was worrying about my surgery, yes. I was also worrying about how much my surgery would cost. Because of the kind of hospital St. Jude was, my family wasn't going to have to pay for my surgery. I had heard my parents talking about bills in low voices when they thought I wasn't listening. I knew that they worked hard but that we weren't rich. So their not having to pay for my treatment was a very big deal.

But who was paying for it?

I kept thinking about all the buildings that made up

the hospital, how many lights there were, how many doctors and nurses. How did they pay for it all?

"Mom," I said from the backseat, "when I get older, I want to raise money for St. Jude."

"You don't have to wait until you get older," Mom said. "You can start now."

I felt like she was right. Kids are powerful too. I didn't have to wait. Now was now.

I got really quiet for a while, thinking about what I wanted to say, and then I asked Mom to turn down the radio.

"I know how to raise money for St. Jude," I told her. "This is the speech I will give: 'My name is Hayley Arceneaux. I had cancer when I was ten years old and came to St. Jude Children's Research Hospital. They saved my leg and my life. If I didn't go there, my family would either go bankrupt or have to sell our house, but we didn't because St. Jude was free. The staff there is very nice, and there isn't one rude or cruel person. When I'm there, I don't think of St. Jude as a cancer hospital but a place where I'm surrounded in love. When people donate, I am very grateful. If you will, please donate money to help pay for the equipment and research to save children's lives.'"

Mom had tears running down her face. I thought it was because my speech was so powerful, but much later, she told me it was because she was hoping and praying I lived through the surgery so that one day I would be able to give that speech.

_____

I woke up after the surgery in the recovery room. The first thing I saw was a physical therapist walking in with a machine that would be used to help make my leg strong again. The machine worked to bend and straighten my leg. Bend and straighten. Bend and straighten. With every bend, with every straighten, I disliked the machine a little bit more.

Physical therapy continued anyway. Three times a week, as part of my recovery, I would go and see the queen of torture, my physical therapist, Lulie.

"Walk pretty," Lulie would say in her Alabama accent.

I would, sometimes cheating and keeping my leg straight as I moved. It was easier to walk without bending my knee, but that left a dramatic limp.

Lulie knew I could do better.

"No, walk pretty," she would say to me, again and again.

Following her directions to walk pretty meant that I was forced to bend my knee with each step. I had less of a limp, but it was a lot harder.

"Again," Lulie would say, even when I was tired. She was hard on me, in the way that I knew she really loved me and wanted me to do well. So many other people were too soft with me during that time, but Lulie knew what I was capable of and how far I could go if I worked hard. Physical therapy was not always fun, but I looked forward to my time with Lulie.

Then one day Lulie was out. Instead, her boss did my lesson. I thought Lulie was tough, but wow. That session was . . . rough. As a result, Lulie was demoted to the princess of pain, and her boss became the new reigning queen of torture.

Over that year, I went from using two crutches to one crutch. Then I let the crutch go, and I found myself walking. I wasn't steady, but I was doing it. And I was doing it on my own. Every time I made one step forward, I rejoiced. Step after shaky step, each one a milestone and a reason to celebrate.

There was a lot to love about life at St. Jude.

The inpatient floor at the hospital had a little juke-box music player, and Hannah and I made the most of it. We dragged our moms and the I.V. poles that held our medications to the hospital library and made flyers with big, colorful fonts that read, "Come watch us dance. The Hayley and Hannah Show."

At night, when nobody was roaming the halls, we put the flyers up all around the hospital. The next morning, the nurses helped us decorate our I.V. poles with paper flowers. Another patient family gave us costumes to wear. Mine was a purple velvet long-sleeved shirt with tassels and bell-bottoms.

At the jukebox, we scanned the song options, but it was easy for me to choose. I always went for the song "All Star" by Smash Mouth.

Showtime, and there was a crowd gathered, including nurses, doctors, other patient families, and Mom. I danced to my opening song, then vomited on the sidelines, sick from my chemo treatments, while Hannah was performing. We performed another song together. Even though I was sick and throwing up between songs, I was still a regular kid and wanted to have some fun.

The crowd cheered loudly. We took our bows and then did an encore, to a lot of applause.

When I wasn't in the hospital, I had many appointments to go to. I hated sitting in the waiting rooms because sitting there was boring and made me feel like a sick kid.

One day I discovered the blood donor room, where adults went to donate blood. When you donate blood, you get a cookie afterward, so I volunteered to hand the cookies out.

I would walk around thanking everyone. "Thank you for donating. If I didn't get blood and platelets, I would shrivel up!"

My job title was "gratitude administrator."

The staff gave me a homemade St. Jude badge to wear. I was very proud to wear it. To me, it meant I was a real employee.

Another way to spend the time between appointments was to join Ms. Penny at the front desk. All her announcements over the intercom were funny and personalized. If a celebrity was coming through, we'd hear Ms. Penny overhead in advance: "Ladies, put on your lipstick."

The two of us were very enthusiastic when it came to greeting people. I would always tell people, "I'm a St. Jude patient, St. Jude fundraiser, and St. Jude employee."

Living in St. Jude housing, there was always something to do to keep me busy. If Hannah and Katie weren't around, I could join the other kids in the common area to play computer games or do arts and crafts. There were volunteers who would come to spend time with us, even a music room where I learned to play piano.

Once a week, a music professor from the local college would come to teach me how to play a complicated song. I couldn't read music, but I memorized the hand motions and I would practice on the keyboard in my apartment for hours. Before going to the hospital, I would play my song over and over again.

By the end of treatment, I had finished learning the whole song.

I was looking forward to going home so much, with one dark cloud: my dog, Chloe. During each of my visits home, I noticed she was moving more slowly and getting sicker. A few months before I finished treatment,

I found out Chloe had died. I was sad, knowing I was going to miss my sweet dog and companion. But I felt peace about it. She had lived a happy, full life, and I had so many wonderful memories with her. I was sure she would want me to have a puppy to keep me company, since she couldn't be there.

Two weeks before I was scheduled to finish treatment, leave St. Jude, and head home, Mom and I decided to go to the Memphis humane society to see the dogs there. That special present she had asked me about during my first surgery was finally going to be mine.

I had decided: I wanted a small, white, fluffy little pup.

Mom and I walked into the adoption center at the exact same time as a woman who was holding the cutest white fluff I had ever seen. She said she was bringing him in to be adopted. I didn't need to look any further than the front door. This was exactly the dog I was looking for! The shelter employee told me that since the pup was so young, I would need to wait two weeks before I could adopt him.

I smiled. Two weeks? Perfect.

My mom had the idea to name my new puppy Cottonball because he resembled a little ball of cotton.

Along with looking forward to getting a puppy at the end of treatment, I had been excited about my "no mo chemo" party all year long. St. Jude has a tradition of throwing a "no mo chemo" party after a patient gets their last dose of chemotherapy. There's even a special song the staff sings at every party.

After my last chemo, I walked into the room, still groggy from the antinausea medication, and was greeted by my favorite staff members. I looked around the room as they sang that special song to me:

Our patients have the cutest S-M-I-L-E.
Our patients have the sweetest H-E-A-R-T.
Oh, we love to see you every day, but now's
the time we get to say . . .
Pack up your bags, get out the door, you don't
get chemo anymore.

It was hard to believe that it was finally happening, but here I was, covered in confetti and Silly String, surrounded by smiling people I loved.

I wanted to cry, but instead I just smiled and laughed. I couldn't cry yet. I had scans coming up in a couple of weeks. I wouldn't be able to go home until we had received news that the tests showed I was free of cancer.

So even though I was full of joy, I held back happy tears.

Scan day. I sat on the exam table waiting for my doctor to come into the room, feeling so nervous. This was it.

This was the moment. *Am I really done? Can I really go home?* This was the most nervous I had been about scans. These had the most riding on them.

It took a long time before my sweet doctor came into the room holding a stack of papers. She sat at her computer and then turned to face me, soft and warm as always.

"Are the scans clear?" I said. I was scared to hear the answer.

She nodded yes.

All the emotions I had been holding inside came out in that moment and I started crying tears of relief. Almost a year of treatment, all of that physical therapy, all of the chemo, all of the vomiting, the loss of my beautiful long hair, it was finally over! I was alive and I was healthy. My difficult cancer journey was done. I had made it. I was clear.

Although I felt relief, I had another feeling I hadn't expected to have: sadness. The truth was that as much as I was looking forward to going home, I was scared to leave this place that had welcomed us, cared for us, protected us, and helped me heal. I was safe here. I was going to miss this place and this family of people I loved and enjoyed seeing every day.

But little fluffy Cottonball was waiting for me, and so were my dad and brother, and so was the rest of my life.

CHAPTER 6

Losing Hope, Choosing Hope

I headed back home to St. Francisville with a lot of hope in my heart. It was going to be a good year, I just knew it. It was such a victory to finish treatment, to see those clear scans.

I wish I could tell you that everything from there on out just got better and better. Well, it didn't.

Nobody knew what to do with me now. I was treated very carefully by nearly every adult I encountered. They constantly asked me how I was feeling and if I needed anything. They would give me gifts. I could do no wrong in their eyes, and they went out of their way to protect me. I missed my St. Jude nurses, who didn't "Bubble Wrap" me. I missed people who made me feel like I was normal.

The one adult in my life who didn't baby me was the one from whom I could have used some help: my fifth-grade teacher.

Especially at the beginning, I had trouble keeping up. Everyone else would be joking around and running off to their next class, and I'd be totally exhausted. She didn't seem to care that I had missed out on the first half of the year and was very late to the game with what they were learning. Or that I was really, really tired. Her class was the first and only class in which I ever got a D on a test.

At the beginning, there were many days when I was too tired to make it through the full day. I'd ask to be excused and go down the hall to my mother's office. "Mom?" I'd say, standing in the doorway. She would look up and give me her soothing smile. It was so good having her there in the building in those moments. She understood what I was going through.

It turned out that finishing treatment didn't mean that I was finished with healing: My life wouldn't go back to normal as fast as my hair would grow back.

A few weeks after I got back to school, the biggest kid in school—the classic male bully—came up to me in the hallway.

"The only reason people are nice to you and like you is because you had cancer," he said, standing over me.

I went to my mom's office and cried.

"Do people like me only because I had cancer?" I asked her, sobbing.

"No," my mom explained. "People like you because you're you. Bullies make up lies to try to bring you down."

I knew that she was right, and it helped. Sort of.

What I needed were friends, but it had been so long since I had seen the girls in my class, and it was starting to feel like we had nothing in common.

At recess one day, I was walking with some girls when one of them brought up Disney World.

"I loved the—" I started to say, excited to share my love of roller coasters.

They walked away before I could finish talking. They were walking so fast I couldn't keep up.

I stood there and stared at their backs, understanding that they hadn't just forgotten about me. They had purposely ditched me. Not one of them looked back to see if I was coming.

I felt like such a loser.

When the school year ended and summer began, I finally had something to look forward to, something that gave me hope that things could get better: Camp Horizon. I couldn't have been any happier to go to the summer sleepaway camp. Camp Horizon is a camp for kids who have or had cancer, set in beautiful rolling hills and woods just outside of Nashville, Tennessee.

Mom and I had been collecting the items on the packing list for weeks. I had my toothbrush and toothpaste, my camera, and all my favorite T-shirts packed into my blue suitcase, which waited in the corner, as excited to go as I was.

Finally, it was mid-June. Mom and I packed up the car and were on our way.

The camp had a swimming pool at one end, a stream flowing into a pond in the middle, cabins throughout, and a large fire circle with logs piled into the firepit right in the middle of camp. It looked like heaven. It quickly became one of my favorite places on Earth.

Our days were full of swimming, arts and crafts, dance, and seeing friends. Each night we came together at the fire circle. We danced to camp songs and made s'mores. We ended each night by singing the Camp Horizon song written by a former camper who had died of cancer, whose chorus went, "Beyond the horizon, there's hope for everyone."

To my great delight, my favorite St. Jude nurse, Lizzie, was the camp nurse that summer, cracking jokes and making me laugh as usual. And best of all? Both Katie and Hannah were there. As usual, they pulled me into their pranks (hello, Silly String). The staff usually allowed them, pretending they didn't know what we were up to.

Being at Camp Horizon went beyond just having fun. It was a place where I could comfortably share feelings that only friends who had cancer truly understood. At home I was embarrassed about my scars; at camp I was able to be around people who had matching ones. Slowly, I was figuring out how to be myself again.

When I was in sixth grade, we went to see Dr. Doom for my regular checkup. My leg had been aching for a while, so I was happy to have him take a look at it. Even physical therapy wasn't helping.

"Hayley," he said, "I'm afraid I've got some bad news."

He explained that the prosthesis had broken.

"What do you mean?" I said. It ached, but I could still walk on it. How could it be broken?

Until that moment, I hadn't worried at all about anything going wrong with the prosthesis. I'd never given a thought to the fact that it could break.

"We have to replace the whole thing," he told me.

I was devastated.

Going through surgery the first time was awful. That second surgery was worse than the first. I spent seventh grade—the year I turned thirteen—in physical therapy. Because our town was so small, we had to drive forty-five minutes to Baton Rouge several times a week for physical therapy after long days of school. Because of all the surgeries, I couldn't bend my knee as much as I used to, which was so frustrating after how hard I had worked to get where I was.

I started at West Feliciana High School the year I turned fifteen. I know there are people for whom high school was absolutely glorious. I am not one of those people.

Freshman year. I tried out for the dance team and didn't make it. *It's okay. I can try again next year,* I told myself.

I was in class a few months later when the teacher said, "Hey, does anyone want to go to the office?"

"I will!" I said.

I stood up to go—and my leg buckled. The pain in my midthigh was unlike anything I had felt before. I could barely walk.

At this point, since I was now in high school, my mom wasn't at the same school as I was. But thankfully she was at the school next door, so she came over immediately when I called her.

I looked at her, tears in my eyes, and said, "I had been doing so well."

Unlike the last time my leg had ached, this time I knew why. My prosthesis was broken.

My third surgery was followed by six long months

on crutches and two and a half years of physical therapy after that. I lost even more ability to bend my knee.
When you're in pain, it's so hard to imagine that anything wonderful might come next.

I felt so down during those days.

Sophomore year. I tried out for the cheerleading team.
When they posted the list of who had made the team,
my name was not on it.

That same evening, I was flying to New Hampshire
for a fundraising event for St. Jude. I spent the flight
trying not to be sad, still feeling the sting of not making
the team.

Traveling to give speeches for St. Jude always made
me feel proud. I was out giving the speech I had written
in my mom's car years earlier, and I loved it! Through
speaking, I was able to help St. Jude *and* get to travel.
The first place we went was New York City. It was a
real adventure to go somewhere new with my family.
Especially to a place that had snow. (Being from the
South, I rarely saw snow.)

That night in New Hampshire, as I gave my speech,
I paid attention to how I felt. I realized that these moments made me feel special, like there actually were
places where I fit in. I told myself: *This is what you're good
at. This is where you're supposed to be.*

———

Even in high school, I knew I wanted to work at St. Jude one day. I was thinking about medicine, which was a challenging career path, so I begged my parents to send me to a new school that would prepare me well for college.

Junior year. I was accepted to St. Joseph's Academy, an all-girls Catholic school in Baton Rouge, just forty-five minutes away. I had my driver's license and a silver car that my parents had gotten for me. I loved that car so much, but it also made me feel a little guilty. Mom and Dad were the kind of parents who drove old cars so they could put the needs and desires of my brother and me first. I recognized what a sacrifice it was for them to send me to that school. Private school was not cheap.

I wanted to show them my appreciation by doing well in school, so I worked and studied harder than I ever had before. Switching schools was a good choice for me. It made me feel powerful because it was something I made happen and got to decide for myself.

This was my fresh start. I could be anyone I wanted.

A girl at my new school found out I had cancer, so I sent her a private Facebook message: "Please don't tell anyone," I wrote.

I didn't want to be labeled as the cancer girl anymore. At that time, I wore only long shorts because I was embarrassed about the scars on my leg. If my shorts slid up my leg when I sat, I would put my hand over my knee to cover the end of my scar with my hand. People probably didn't notice, but I was always very aware of it. I had a complicated relationship with my leg. I would always call it "my bad leg."

It took time to get to that place where I could say, "I love my scars." I had to heal, and I had to see things in a new light.

Through the years, I learned how to accept myself. The way I see it now, I have two good legs. Do they look different? Yeah, they do. Do I wear short shorts now? Yeah, I do! I learned to appreciate that my leg has worked so hard and overcome so much. It's gotten me to where I need to be.

I also learned to be proud of my cancer journey. Instead of seeing having had cancer as a weakness and something I was embarrassed about, I began to see it as something that made me powerful and special. Even though I had to go through an experience that not many other people my age could relate to, I realized that my journey made me the strong person I am. And it gave me a unique and beautiful perspective on living life.

I'm so proud of this leg and of my journey. And I'm so grateful to the people who helped me get here: After I graduated from high school, I mailed a letter to my old physical therapist Lulie, the princess of pain, telling her that it was thanks to her that I walked across the graduation stage in high heels.

CHAPTER 7

Trains, Planes—and Spain!

I had been so excited to go to college—and I was right to feel that way. College was *awesome*. At Southeastern Louisiana University, all my best friends were just a few steps away at all times.

In my freshman year, I joined a sorority, an all-girls organization on campus, because I wanted to get involved and make some new friends. I even got a "big sis," someone who could show me what being part of a sorority was all about. A year later, I had my own "little sis," a freshman named Gabrielle. The moment we met, we clicked. There's nothing like the feeling of making a great new friend, and Gabrielle became that for me.

College was a time when I got to know so many new people—and got to know new parts of myself. I definitely wanted to have fun in college. If there was a costume party or a football game, I was there. I joined every club I could. But I was even more serious about my grades. Since I was still focused on working at St. Jude one day, there were many nights I would force myself to leave my friends and go to the library to study.

Still, even with my dedication to studying, I got to spend so many hours sitting on the comfy couches of the sorority house watching movies and making memories with the other girls. These were my soulmates, those best-friendships that you know are lifelong. These relationships showed me that I could be my silly self and still be loved and accepted.

The summer after my freshman year, I took an internship in the fundraising department at St. Jude. While I was there, I made a new friend named Luis. Luis and I had so much in common that we couldn't help but become friends. We were just about the same age, had the same cancer, had the same type of prosthesis, and had the same beloved Dr. Doom.

His family was from Honduras and spoke Spanish, but they had come to the United States for Luis's treatment. That summer, through his family's experience, I saw how hard it was for people to go through cancer treatment when English wasn't their first language.

Luis liked to play guitar and sing. He was always

thinking about the younger kids with cancer back in Honduras and would collect toys to take to them. He was a special person, always thinking of others.

Becoming friends with his family gave me the idea to study Spanish along with studying science, so that I could one day work with Spanish-speaking patient families in their native language.

When I got back to school, I changed my college major to Spanish.

My Spanish classes quickly became my favorite courses. I felt like I was learning a secret language that would help me talk with new people in a new way. The best part of studying Spanish was that I got to go to Spain the next summer with some of my classmates and teachers. I loved it so much and promised myself I would return.

With Spanish, it felt like my whole world was opening up.

In my senior year, I went back to Spain, this time by myself.

My mom, who had been to Europe in high school, encouraged me to go. Dad agreed it was a great idea. He had spent his high school years in Greece. They both believed in the importance of travel, so much so that they went ahead and bought that plane ticket to Spain for me. I appreciated their support so much.

I was so excited for that trip. I felt so brave about

traveling by myself, so ready to conquer the world. That is, up until the minute I had to say goodbye to Dad at the airport. It was way harder than I thought it would be.

On the plane, I wondered what I was thinking, leaving behind everyone and everything I knew.

I lived in Spain for the fall semester with a host family. Eva was a single mom and her daughters, Paula and Marta, were in middle school. Eva would often do small, kind things for me. I didn't like waking up early (I still don't), but she would make sandwiches for my lunch every day, wrap them up, and leave them outside my bedroom door. Every morning I would open my door to fresh sandwiches with the best Spanish ingredients. How spoiled was I?

I was an extremely picky eater, so Eva tried to make foods I liked but also encouraged me to try new things. I ate salad and fish for the first time in Spain. Yes, it's true that I had never tried regular green salad or even fish before I went to Spain.

Often I didn't know what the foods were.

"*Queso de cabra* is good!" I would say.

"That's goat cheese," Eva would explain.

Goat? I would think. *Glad I didn't know that!*

Everything in Spain was just a little bit different, from the signs in Spanish to the way you flushed the toilet by pressing a button instead of pressing down a lever. Speaking in my second language, I had to think so much harder to order a meal, buy stamps, or simply get around. In my small town back home, we didn't have any public transportation, but in Spain, I learned to enjoy riding the metro, their subway system.

For a twenty-one-year-old American sorority girl, living in a completely new culture was not always easy. My host family was so nice, but others were not always patient as I was learning the language.

The experience gave me a whole new appreciation for what people who speak English as a second language go through in the United States. I appreciated their courage in such a new and deep way. I was determined that once I got back home, I was going to do anything I could to make them feel welcome, especially in my future work as a physician assistant.

Over time, I found my way in Spain. I met other study-abroad students and we went out for dinner and enjoyed all the best Spanish food, like paella, the best rice dish I ever had. I still order paella whenever I see it on a menu; the taste transports me right back to my time in Spain.

Traveling with my new friends helped me to see such a special beauty in other cultures and appreciate in a whole new way people who were different from me. I went to twelve European countries that semester, and I saw myself become more outgoing and confident, more open-minded and less judgmental. I eased into the go-with-the-flow attitude because I started to see that things usually had a way of working out. If I took the wrong train in the metro system, I learned I could just look at a map and find my way back, with or without the help of the locals.

In Spain, everyone was always telling me to calm down: "No pasa nada." "Tranquila." It took me a while to adapt to Spain's laid-back lifestyle. They must have been getting something right, because the people certainly seemed less stressed.

I still remind myself of what I learned in Spain when I feel unsure or worried, or when I'm running late to the airport.

Tranquila, I tell myself. *No pasa nada.*

CHAPTER 8

Peru

I wish I could tell you that I loved physician assistant school as much as I loved college, but I did not love it. PA school is so hard and so fast, it's basically medical school in two years instead of four.

I spent my nights up late studying and spent weekends in the library. I never forgot my motivation for all of the hard work. I wanted to work with kids with cancer, and nothing was going to stop me. I was always the one with my nose in a book, always studying, always trying my hardest.

Part of PA school involved clinical rotations, where we spent time in all of the departments of the hospital. Finally, I got to interact with patients. It was great—until it came time for my emergency department rotation. I had been dreading that experience so much. I was sure I was going to hate the ED.

The morning I was supposed to begin, I called Mom and told her that I wished I didn't have to do it at all.

Throughout my ED rotation, patients would come in with all kinds of problems that felt like a puzzle I could solve. I would meet with them and listen to their problems, order tests, order them medicine, and help them. And it all happened within a few hours, because the ED is so fast-paced.

It was nothing like what I expected. I loved it!

I learned you just never know what will work for you unless you try it.

I was getting close to finishing PA school when two PA jobs became available at St. Jude. I was so excited and applied for both of them. I wrote heartfelt letters telling them that a job at St. Jude was my dream. I felt very confident. *Of course* this was going to work out. I was supposed to work at St. Jude. Right?

Wrong.

I didn't even get an interview.

I was so disappointed. I had been studying for this and working so hard for so many years, and I wasn't even considered for the job.

If there's one thing kids with cancer get used to, it's disappointment. So I had a good crying session, and then I moved on. It helped that I had been offered a great job at an emergency department in Baton Rouge, which I happily accepted. I loved the excitement and energy of the ED. If I needed to gain some experience, where better to do it than in a busy emergency department?

Before starting at the ED, I volunteered for a month in a rural clinic in Peru.

Mom and Dad brought me to the airport. Of course, that just made it harder to say goodbye.

I pulled my parents into a tight hug. The three of us stood there for a moment.

"I'm sorry," I told them. "I know my adventures make you nervous. Thank you for always supporting me no matter what."

Once again, I was by myself, going to a country where I didn't know anyone.

What am I getting myself into?

Fourteen hours later, I landed at the airport in Peru and was taken to volunteer headquarters, where we were given information about our host families. I was placed with a roommate, a nurse from Australia named Renee, who was going to be volunteering with me in the same clinic for the same amount of time. Perfect!

My host mom was always feeding me way more than I could eat, offering me huge platefuls of rice, beans, potatoes, and chicken. A few years had passed since I was the picky eater in Spain. I was much more adventurous now, though I still couldn't bring myself to try the local dish of guinea pig.

Renee and I ventured out together to explore the city and I fell in love with the historic architecture, the local markets, and the friendly, welcoming people. When we weren't at the clinic, we walked for miles around the city. On the weekends, we traveled around the country.

When it came to exploring, I was ready to go. But it was a little scary to start working as a brand-new PA, let alone in an unfamiliar place, teaching people healthcare in my second language.

Each morning my roommate and I would take a bus to a different part of the city and wait for someone to go by in a van yelling, "Chinchero" (the name of the rural town where we were working). We would hop into the crowded van with the locals. The views along that hour-long drive were beautiful, with large fields and tall mountains. We also passed homes that were on the verge of crumbling. Many homes did not have electricity. Poverty was all around us. Each day reminded me more and more how fortunate I was.

We would study Spanish during the drive to the clinic. My roommate was learning Spanish for the first time, so she was studying the basics, especially numbers, since she would be reporting vital signs. I was given lists of vocabulary specific to Peru to study, as well as medical words.

The clinic was simple and lacked many basic resources. Wild dogs would even run through the clinic at times. Even so, I was impressed by the staff's creativity in managing. Seeing them build a homemade wheelchair out of a lawn chair with wheels bolted on was inspiring.

They treated all ages, even delivering babies in the back room. The clinic also had an in-house pharmacy so patients could pick up their medications.

For a month, I cared for patients, took their information in Spanish, diagnosed their illnesses, and wrote prescriptions for medications to help them feel better. Thanks to my Spanish, I could learn things and get to know people I couldn't have otherwise known.

People didn't seem to question the fact that I was clearly speaking to them in my second language, with my strong American accent that I still can't shake. Even when I knew I was making tons of errors and stumbling on words, I was often told, "Wow, your Spanish is so good!"

That encouragement went a long way in giving me confidence and making me want to keep trying.

They also didn't seem to mind the long waits to be seen. But I did. My experience in Peru taught me more than ever that everyone deserves good medical care, no matter where on Earth they live or how old or how young they are. It's something I fight for to this day.

CHAPTER 9

Saying Goodbye

I finished up my volunteer work in Peru and headed back to the United States, where I was finally able to start my new job in the emergency department. I even volunteered to work all the night shifts. Working in the ED was incredible. The work was fast-paced and satisfying. The schedule was flexible, which meant that it allowed me time for my favorite hobby, travel.

Then, about a year into my new job, my dad started complaining of new pains. For as long as I could remember, he had been on a diet. He always wanted to lose weight but usually didn't (because he was always cheating and sneaking Popsicles). Suddenly, his clothes were too loose on him. With these new symptoms and because of my training as a PA, I was very worried.

"Dad," I said, "you need to see your doctor. Tell him I said that I'm worried you have cancer."

He hugged me.

"It could be a million different things," he said.

"I know," I said. "But we need to make sure."

I had such a bad feeling, like a pit in my stomach. I just couldn't shake it.

Dad scheduled a test, and it confirmed my biggest fear. He had cancer, with a big tumor on his kidney and little tumors throughout his body.

I was devastated. I didn't sleep at all that night. I was out of town, and the next morning I flew home and went straight from the airport to the hospital.

It was so strange to see Dad in a hospital gown, the same gown my patients in the ED wore. They were my sick patients, and he was my healthy, strong dad. My brain just couldn't put those two things together.

When Dad was diagnosed, I promised to take my parents on an international trip, hoping it would give us something to look forward to during a dark time. That's what the idea of travel does for me, maybe as much as the actual going. Thinking about the amazing places that exist in the world can help elevate you above your circumstances. It can give you hope.

Dad was too sick to go. I needed something joyous to hold on to in the moment.

I thought, *I'm going to get a puppy.*

That was when I got Scarlett. In my family, when someone has cancer, we get puppies. We believe in looking forward, in rejoicing, even when our heart is breaking, even when we're grieving.

We were by Dad's side for the next seven months as they tried chemo and radiation. Unfortunately, his cancer was aggressive and couldn't be stopped.

We spent Dad's last days having long talks and sharing what was most important.

He said, "The most important things in life are family and showing love. I don't know how much time I have left, but I will continue showing love."

We asked him what he thought we would miss most about him, and he said his humor. He was right about that, among so many other things.

My mother was amazing. She was losing her husband and best friend, and she was still our family rock more than ever. My dad was so grateful to her, calling her his saint. He told us to listen to her and said that he couldn't have imagined a better family or a more wonderful partner.

The next morning, my mom came into my room in tears and said, "I think he's gone."

I grabbed my stethoscope and went in to listen to Dad's heart, but I heard no heartbeat. I felt no pulse. He was gone.

A few hours later it was raining while the sun was out. For some reason, I took that as a sign that he was okay.

Dad's funeral was in a beautiful church with beautiful flowers and beautiful music. Hayden and I did Dad's eulogy. Dad was the town journalist, and everyone knew and loved him. When he passed, the whole town came to pay their respects and honor his incredible life.

After the funeral, I told my mom she could choose anywhere in the world to go and I would take her. She picked Italy and Switzerland, and I took two weeks off work to travel with her. We started in Venice. Of course, we rode through the canals in gondolas because in Venice, you just have to.

From there we headed to Cinque Terre to meet Hayden and his wife, Liz. We took a pesto-making cooking class with a view of the colorful, historic buildings on the mountainside overlooking the Mediterranean. We swam at a rocky beach. We kayaked. A local man took us on his boat and we swam in perfectly clear green-blue water. At Lake Como, we explored the towns along the lake and went to the top of one of the mountains to see the full panoramic view.

The best part? We spent so much of our time together just laughing, even when my mom tripped and fell (after we found out she was okay, of course). And we shared so many stories about Dad.

Mom was so happy, at peace. Dad would have wanted that for her more than anything, for her to feel so loved.

CHAPTER 10

Full Circle

After three years working in the ED, I felt in my gut it was finally time to go get my dream job at St. Jude. At the same time, an opportunity presented itself that was just perfect for me.

This time, I got the interview.

The day before my twenty-eighth birthday, I drove to Memphis for the big interview I had waited years to get. I met with so many people.

"This is my dream job," I told them all.

Mom called as I was driving home. "Hey, birthday girl," she said. "How was it?"

"So good," I said. "So good!"

I had spent the past two years since Dad's death traveling and working in the ED. I did yoga in Mexico, camped in the Sahara Desert in Morocco, hiked on a glacier in New Zealand. Traveling brought me so much joy. New languages, food, cultures. I wanted to experience it all.

Now that I had visited more than twenty countries, I felt it was the right time to start work at St. Jude.

I was sure I'd be moving to Memphis soon. It was my time, this time.

The second I woke up the next day, the morning of my birthday, I checked the St. Jude website to see if there were any updates.

What I saw was a big "no" glaring me in the face. I hadn't gotten the job.

I spent the day ugly crying. All I wanted was to work at St. Jude.

How could I not have gotten my *dream* job?

I told myself to stop crying. I wasn't giving up. I would find a way.

A week later, I got an email from St. Jude telling me they had a job they thought I'd be perfect for. I applied right away.

From the Memphis airport, I called Mom. "Do you remember eighteen years ago when we were here and I said, 'Who would ever want to live in Memphis?'"

"Yes," she said.

"Well," I laughed, "now I'm praying harder than ever that I'll get to live in Memphis."

I had another long day of interviews. I felt such a

spark with the inpatient leukemia and lymphoma team. I was inspired by the way they spoke about their passion for the job and how they were able to help the patients and families. I felt at home.

I met with my old nurse Lizzie in the cafeteria before I flew back.

"Good luck," she said. "I believe in you."

Every day, I waited to hear something. Nothing. I was constantly checking my email and trying to shake my nerves, but nothing could take away how anxious I felt. Finally, a week later, I got my answer.

I did it. I got my dream job.

I ugly cried again, this time with overwhelming joy. Finding out I got my dream job was the happiest moment of my life. Working at St. Jude was all I ever wanted. The job wasn't just given to me; I had to work hard for it. All those years of studying and working so hard and hoping. All of it was worth it.

Back at St. Jude again, this time as a PA, everything made sense. I was exactly where I was supposed to be. Instead of a patient bracelet on my arm, this time I had an employee ID badge around my neck.

My days were full. By 7:00 A.M. I was at work, talking to the kids and hearing their problems and examining them. At 9:30 A.M., I would have rounds with the doctors, nurses, and medical staff to talk about what problems our patients were going through, what medicines they needed, what the plan was. Later, I'd go and talk the plan through with the families and answer all their questions.

Throughout the day, more patients would be admitted to the hospital, some coming to St. Jude for the very first time.

"I've been there too," I would tell them. "And I know one thing: Having cancer will change your life in a lot of good ways. Plus, you're going to make some awesome friends while you're here."

Since my first days at St. Jude, I'd viewed Memphis as my city. Now it truly was.

When I moved to Memphis in April 2020, it was just a month after the COVID-19 pandemic began. Scarlett and I would take long walks to explore in our free time.

At first, Scarlett and I lived in an apartment. A few months later, I found a white brick house that I knew was perfect for us. It had bedrooms for my friends to stay in and all the charm of an older home. I fell in love. Plus, it had a nice backyard for Scarlett.

Everything was finally fitting together perfectly.

In many ways, I believe that having cancer has been my greatest gift, something I learned over time. Childhood cancer gave my life purpose and gave me a sense of adventure. I have such a love for life because of my cancer journey. I appreciate the healthy days more than

I ever would have before. I love every day that I'm alive and getting to experience as much as I can of what life has to offer.

I love the unexpectedness of life. I love that things work out. You have to hold on, even on the hard days, because you don't know what great thing can come and change your life.

Anything can happen.

Part 2

Dreams

You'll never know if you don't go (go!)
—Smash Mouth, "All Star"

CHAPTER 11

The Magic Dragon

Just as I was getting adjusted to my new life, I got The Call.

The Call. My invitation to go to space. That call changed everything.

All I had ever wanted was to be back at St. Jude. Going to space wasn't something I could have even imagined wanting. But the moment they asked me, more than anything else in the world, I wanted to go.

A few days after The Call was my first Zoom call with Jared, the guy who would be taking me to space. I was at work and went into an empty interactive room with a waterfall on the screen behind me so I looked like I was in a Costa Rican jungle.

What if I meet this guy and he doesn't like me and picks someone else to go to space? That was my biggest worry.

I had known about the mission for only three days, and my heart was already so set on going.

I joined the call, and there they were: Jared Isaacman, the guy I had been googling all week, and Kidd Poteet, the man who would be our mission director and serve as the behind-the-scenes person helping us get to space.

Jared was younger than I'd imagined, with the most genuine smile. He had been described to me as this billionaire businessman CEO fighter jet pilot; but there, talking to me on the screen, was a really normal, hilarious guy. His good friend Kidd, an ex-Thunderbird military pilot (he had been in the U.S. Air Force), was grinning too. Their friendly expressions put me at ease.

Jared outlined the basic details of the mission, starting with the name: Inspiration4, because the four crew members were on a mission to inspire the world. The amazing thing was that the whole crew would be made up of civilians. Jared had his pilot's license, but he wasn't an astronaut, and he had never trained for or been to space.

Our mission's goal was to raise $200 million for St. Jude. *Wow!* It was the biggest fundraiser the hospital had ever seen. Jared was donating too: $125 million. Everyone always asks if he created this mission because he has a personal relationship with childhood cancer. He doesn't; he just hates childhood cancer and wants to see it cured.

I had prepared a list of questions, this time with the help of my brother so that I didn't ask silly questions like whether we were going to the moon. Jared was so approachable and easy to talk to, not the intimidating billionaire I had in mind.

The company sending us to space was called SpaceX, and Jared invited me to come out to their facility in California the next week so I could start my medical evaluations and get fitted for my space suit.

"It'll be the most intense set of measurements you'll ever have taken," he said. "Two hundred and twenty measurements, to be exact."

Then he smiled even bigger. He told me that while we were in space we were going to be able to talk live with St. Jude patients and their families. I would be able to bring all my patients into that moment with me. I thought about how much hope it would give those cancer-fighting kids watching it, as well as their parents.

These kids can do anything! That was the message I was determined to send them.

Kidd texted me as soon as the call was over so I would have his number. He said they would pick me up in Memphis the next week to head to SpaceX.

"Pick me up?"

"Private plane," he explained.

That was a new concept for me. Okay, it was all new for me.

———

I was to meet up with Jared and Kidd in Memphis's small private airport, and I had been told that a film crew would be there to capture the moment. Our journey was going to be filmed and made into a documentary.

After a morning of work at St. Jude, I ran home, quickly curled my hair, and changed out of my scrubs. I made it to the airport just in time. A small plane covered in black and gray swirls touched down.

"That's Jared's plane," someone told me.

I stood just inside the door while a sound man put a microphone on me; two cameras were facing me, with a sound boom overhead. As if I needed any more reasons to be nervous in that moment!

Jared and Kidd walked up, both wearing Inspiration4 vests over T-shirts, jeans, and tennis shoes, what I would come to call "the Jared uniform." In my black dress and square-heeled white leather boots, I felt overdressed.

The film crew stood behind us.

"Hello!" Jared and Kidd called out, smiling broadly.

Jared was even taller than I had imagined, a contrast to my five-foot-two stature. He was so friendly, and yet I felt so awkward. The microphone pinned to my neckline wasn't helping.

We were led to a conference room, where there was a spread of Memphis barbecue waiting for us. The food looked good, but I was nervous and barely touched it. An hour later, it was time to go.

"Nice plane," I told Jared as we climbed the stairs, ready to head to California.

"Even though the design looks like Mike Tyson's face tattoo," he said.

I laughed. "Now I can't unsee it," I said.

Okay, he's cool, I thought. *This is going to be okay.*

The next morning, Kidd drove us from our hotel in LA to Hawthorne, where SpaceX was located. I was impressed by the collection of tall white buildings and the large rocket booster looming over the front door. It was incredible to see. Here they were making Dragon capsules like the one I would be taking to space, and other rocket parts.

I was given a tour of the facilities. We walked through the rocket factory and into the astronaut training room, where I was going to be fitted for my space suit.

"Try these on," someone said, handing me a pile of clothes.

I went into the changing room and slid into a tight black long-sleeved shirt, tights, and socks to wear for the fitting.

Once changed, I was greeted by a team of space suit engineers.

"I'm Maria," said a blond Swedish woman with a

tape measure around her neck. Before working for SpaceX, Maria had helped create superhero costumes for movies. It certainly felt like I was being measured for superhero gear.

The process took hours. My hands and feet were traced, and all the different angles were measured. Maria wrapped the tape measure around every inch of my arms, legs, and torso and read the numbers aloud, 220 measurements in all.

She handed me a space suit helmet to try on. I slid it over my head, suddenly in a world separate from everyone around me, all outside sounds muffled. I turned my head from left to right, looking around, getting a feel for it.

Next the team fitted me for my seat in the capsule, taking care to get the width and height of the seat just right to make sure that I'd be comfortable for the long hours before liftoff.

Later in the day, Jared joined me in the astronaut training room. We went and sat in our training capsule, an exact replica of the Dragon capsule that would be our spacecraft.

"This is where we're going to live for three days," he said.

"Home sweet home," I replied.

The next day, I met with SpaceX's main doctor, Anil, and provided him with my medical history. He and three other physicians did a basic physical exam, listening to my heart and lungs, looking in my ears, feeling the lymph nodes of my neck, and walking me through a neurological exam.

At one point I was asked to flap my hands back and forth, and I did so quickly.

One of the physicians laughed. "Wow, you're fast."

I said, "Gotta go to space!"

Two weeks later, I was back for more medical evaluations. When some of my tests came back abnormal, more tests were added. Hearing the word "abnormal" made me want to cry.

I was frightened, but I didn't want to look weak in front of the SpaceX physicians. Astronauts have to be strong, and I needed them to give me the green light.

I endured test after test, until I was finally medically cleared for space flight.

My first win.

CHAPTER 12

Inspirati④n

When Jared announced the first all-civilian mission to space, my involvement in it was still a secret. Ultimately, the four Inspiration4 crew members would each represent a different pillar of inspiration. Since Jared would be the commander of the mission, he was representing "Leadership." As the St. Jude ambassador, I was representing "Hope."

All he revealed in this first big announcement was that he was leading the mission and that the "Hope" seat had been filled by a former St. Jude patient currently working for the hospital. He used the pronoun "she." That was all he said about me.

At that point, only two of four crew members had been selected—Jared and me. We didn't get to pick who would be selected as our fellow crew members.

"Generosity" would go to someone who had entered a lottery by donating to St. Jude. (My friend Gabrielle entered a *lot* of times.)

"Prosperity" would go to the winner of a contest: Anyone who ran a business through Jared's website Shift4Shop could enter by making a Twitter video about who they were and what they did.

I hadn't told anyone I worked with about the mission, but even though Jared left my name out of it, they put it together. Within hours, my co-workers were texting me, telling me how happy they were for me. They didn't ask if I was the one going; they just knew. I just shrugged and smiled.

A few weeks before my announcement as the second crew member, Jared gave me the go-ahead to tell a few close friends my news. Lauren was coming to Memphis for the weekend, and I mentioned that I had some big news to share.

Along with being my cousin, Lauren is my very favorite person and best friend. She always has been. Now she was standing in my guest bedroom doing her makeup in the mirror. I looked at her applying mascara, pursing her mouth and raising her eyebrows as she waved the wand near her face.

"Well," she said, "are you going to tell me your news?"

"Yeah," I said. "It's kind of crazy. I'm going to outer space."

She yelped and spun toward me, nearly painting a stripe down her cheek in the process.

"I could cry," she said as I explained more about the mission. "I'm proud of you. I'm nervous. But I'm just so proud."

I told my other closest friends that I had a big secret, and we made a FaceTime date.

I started the conversation by asking if they had any guesses.

"Dating show?" said one.

"Nope," I said. I hated to disappoint, but no, I was not going to be on *The Bachelor*.

Finally, I told them the truth.

"Wait, *what?*"

"No way."

"You've got to be kidding."

They were absolutely stunned when I told them I was going to be an astronaut. And to be honest, I was still feeling pretty stunned myself.

A month later, on February 22, from a laptop in Jared's New York City apartment, with the skyline of Midtown Manhattan in the background, I told the world I was going to space. I had too many follow-up interviews to count.

At the end of the day, I had hundreds and hundreds of unread texts and messages. It felt like everyone I'd ever known reached out that day to express their shock and excitement for me. I just felt so happy.

Before the announcement, especially when I was going through the extensive medical evaluations, I was so worried that the opportunity would somehow slip away and no one would have ever known. Now the world knew. I didn't have to keep the secret to myself anymore.

I was going to be an astronaut.

In every interview I gave about going to space, I was asked what I was looking forward to the most. Every time, I said that it was the call from space with the St. Jude patients.

By early March, we knew who our two other crew members were going to be.

"Generosity" was Chris Sembroski, who won out over seventy-two thousand other people. Even more incredible was that it was actually one of his friends who'd won the seat on Inspiration4. That guy couldn't go, and so he gave his seat to Chris.

"Prosperity" was Dr. Sian Proctor, a geoscientist and community college professor who had set up her space-themed art and poetry website, Space2Inspire, through

Jared's company. She won the Twitter video contest. What a prize!

In late March, we all went to Cape Canaveral in Florida to announce to the world our full Inspiration4 crew. I liked my other crew members immediately. From the moment we met, Sian had the kind of confidence and warmth I would come to see was her signature.

Chris hugged me when we were introduced. "I'm so excited!" he said, and then he hugged me again.

I was able to bring a plus-one to our full-crew announcement. "Hayden," I said, "will you come with me?" I knew he would appreciate the space history of Cape Canaveral and geek out on the tour.

"YES!" he said.

It was good to have my brother by my side as we toured the launchpad.

"Do you see that?" he said, pointing at a sprinkler. "I modeled that in college."

I felt so proud of him.

"My brother modeled that!" I kept saying.

We toured the Falcon 9 rocket factory, and I made mental notes as the team pointed out the different stages of the rocket and how it would all work together to take us to orbit.

Hayden asked the engineers technical question after technical question.

"What type of propellant do the engines use?"

"How many engines can you lose and still make it to orbit?"

Normally I would have told him to stop with the millions of questions, but I knew he was getting all the information he needed to feel this rocket was safe enough for his big sister.

In the days prior to the full crew announcement, we were filmed and interviewed together. I was so excited that we were a diverse crew. Half the crew was female, Sian is Black, and I would be the first person in space with a prosthetic body part, as well as the first pediatric cancer survivor and the youngest American.

I loved hearing Sian's and Chris's backstories and how they each had a lifelong passion for space. Several years earlier, Sian had applied to be a NASA astronaut and made it all the way to the finals. That time, she didn't get to go. Now, finally, she was going to be an astronaut.

She smiled as she told me her story. I just wanted to be her best friend.

I was also getting to know Chris, a former Space Camp counselor, former air force member, current engineer, and dad. He possessed no shortage of dad jokes.

Then there was Jared. Over the past months, our

relationship had taken on a brother/sister vibe. I loved that he could make me crack up, and he also had a thoughtful side to him.

I felt like I'd known each of them for years, even though we were just getting started.

Immediately following the announcement, we flew from Cape Canaveral to Pennsylvania to start training. On the plane, my new crewmates and I were handed a thousand posters to sign for donors who had supported our fundraising mission. With each slash of my pen, I wondered why anyone would care about my autograph.

We chatted while we signed. Jared kept reminding us that we had to prove ourselves in order to be signed off by SpaceX to fly on the mission. Being at SpaceX and doing the training didn't mean we were going. Up to that point, being chosen just meant that we got to try.

If we wanted to actually get to space, we would have to earn it.

First up, the centrifuge.

CHAPTER 13

G-Monster

Our first training exercise was in something called the centrifuge.

Here's what I knew about centrifuges, thanks to my summer internship in college doing lab research for St. Jude. Part of my work was analyzing genetic material. It was my job to extract DNA by running it through a centrifuge.

A centrifuge works by spinning whatever you put in it so intensely that centrifugal force begins to act upon it. Since the DNA in our cells has a lighter molecular weight than the other cellular stuff, like proteins, when the centrifuge spins around, the lighter stuff and the heavier stuff separate. It's like a blender that works in reverse, as if you could take a milkshake and turn it back into Oreos and vanilla ice cream.

Just think about how powerful your blender is. The centrifuge is that and more. So powerful that during that summer, every time I put a vial into the centrifuge, I stepped back and away from the force of that whirl.

Now I was being asked to get inside of one.

The moment I first heard about the centrifuge, before we even got to Cape Canaveral for the big crew announcement, I flashed back to being fifteen and the way my leg buckled when my prosthesis broke. The two years it took to heal were excruciating, and while I'll need a new prosthesis someday, it's not something I like to think about or talk about.

Cancer is something I had. I got better. I don't have cancer anymore. What I do still have, what I'll always have, is a rod in my leg that I worry could break at any moment. And now I was going to take my leg into highly stressful conditions, on purpose.

Consider that Earth gravity has a G-force of one. You can't feel it, but it's strong enough to keep you from floating away. The centrifuge was going to be my first introduction to six Gs, or six times the normal amount of gravity.

If my rod could break when I simply stood up, if I was already worried about slipping and hurting myself during a light drizzle outside, what could the centrifuge do to me?

I asked Kidd, "Do you know of anyone else who's done centrifuge training with a prosthetic body part?"

"Nope."

"Cool."

On the outside, I was all confidence. Of course I could do it! No problem! Bring on the G-forces!

But on the inside, I was scared. I wanted reassurance. If only someone could tell me my leg would be okay.

I was at home about a week before we started training, and I went to visit Dr. Doom, who had reached out to say he had a gift for me.

It had been a while, and it was really nice to see him. He presented me with an official St. Jude orthopedics sweatshirt.

Then I asked him the question that had been burning up my mind. "Do you think it's going to be okay for me to do centrifuge training? Can my leg handle all those G-forces?" I trusted him to be real with me, as he always had been.

"Probably," Dr. Doom said.

I breathed a sigh of relief. A "probably" from him is like a big smile plus a high five from somebody else.

Then he said, "But . . ."

. . . and he picked up one of the prosthesis models he had on his shelf.

"Your prosthesis can bend this way," said Dr. Doom,

showing me the normal movements of the prosthesis. "And it can bend this way."

I nodded.

"The problem is if it goes like this." And he separated the prosthesis in two, holding the pieces apart widely.

I thought I was going to throw up. This was my absolute worst nightmare. "That can't happen," I said. "If that happens, I will die."

His nurse practitioner, whom I've known for years, is a woman I really respect. "Dr. Neel," she said, "that isn't going to happen. She has bone holding it in, and muscle, and skin."

She turned to me. "Hayley, your leg is *not* going to split in two."

At least one of us was sure.

We got to the hotel in Pennsylvania the evening before centrifuge training, and I fell asleep quickly, exhausted from the last few days. As I was drifting off to sleep, I thought about what the next day would bring. Hayley versus the centrifuge. This would be my first real activity with my new team, our first astronaut training. This was where we would show one another what we were made of, and I was determined to show them how tough I was.

My butterflies flew away in the morning light, replaced by adrenaline and excitement as I stepped into my brand-new flight suit that I was to wear to my training activities. I had never worn anything like it. The material was thick and hadn't been broken in yet, and it was covered in zippers. I kept discovering pockets I hadn't noticed before.

I looked in the mirror. I looked so fierce in that suit. This unbelievable getup was the most amazing thing I had ever seen myself in. I am a person who loves a costume; my friends and I have been known to wear tutus and fun Mardi Gras outfits. But this was something else. Not pretend. Not dress-up. All real. There's nothing like a flight suit to remind you that you've got what it takes. The confidence boost was through the roof.

Our energy in the car on the drive over to the building that housed the centrifuge was really loud and all over the place. We were all talking and laughing, riding this wave of excitement.

"I want to talk with you guys about something," Jared said, cutting through the energy in the car with his firmest "I'm serious" tone. One thing about Jared is that he can be very funny, but when he is serious, he means it.

"You've all been selected, but we still have to *earn* our spots," he reminded us again. "SpaceX will not fly us if we're not ready."

We all got really quiet. I took a breath and told myself to focus. Jared was a fighter jet pilot. Sian was a geoscientist and private pilot. Chris had been in the air force. And then there was me, the youngest and the smallest, and the one who had the prosthesis. I reminded myself that I was the medical officer of the mission. I belonged here. I was bringing my own experience, and they needed me.

I knew it. I just needed them to know it.

The centrifuge was in a massive room with large windows for maximum viewing pleasure—the pleasure of the viewer, not of the person being centrifuged, obviously. The machine itself was basically a little capsule attached to a motor that would spin it all around the room. They gave us a quick tour, and then we went into a classroom to learn the physics of G-forces and what to expect with launch (leaving Earth) and reentry (coming back to Earth).

We would be going into the centrifuge one by one: first Jared, then Chris, then Sian, and finally me.

Jared climbed into the capsule. I looked through the windows as the small capsule he was in began to hurl around, whipping through the space at an alarming speed. There was also a monitor set up that allowed us to watch what was happening inside the centrifuge.

I could see Jared's face twisting under the power of

this strange new pressure. When he hit high G-forces, I could see how hard he was concentrating on breathing. We had been taught techniques that would keep our lungs inflated despite all that pressure on our chests.

SpaceX had designed the machine so that we could feel and learn to adapt to launch and reentry G-forces. The experience can be uncomfortable and claustrophobic, so it's an important part of training.

I was not too thrilled to be going last. Mostly because I hate waiting.

Next up was Chris. Who threw up. And then gave us a thumbs-up to let us know he was okay.

Sian gave me a reassuring hug before she slipped out the door. Then only I was left, just me and my thoughts.

Finally it was my turn. I walked into the room in my flight suit, channeling that fierce feeling as I climbed into the centrifuge. The interior of the capsule looked like you'd imagine a spaceship, with a flight seat, a pretend control deck, and a G-force meter.

I sat down and strapped in, thinking about the centrifuge in the St. Jude lab. Now I was the test sample.

My Apple watch registered my heartbeat, which was really fast. I took a deep breath and looked for my calm. I wasn't there only for me. I was there for something bigger.

Instead of focusing on what I was afraid of—pain, the unknown—I focused on the larger picture and the real reason I was there. *I have to do this,* I told myself. *Not just for me. For everyone coming after me.* This wasn't about this centrifuge or this exercise. It was about going to space. It was about representing people who weren't physically perfect. In order for more people with prosthetics to follow in my footsteps, first I would have to get to space.

I felt like there was a lot riding on my shoulders, but in a beautiful, empowering way.

They turned the centrifuge on and the whole capsule shifted its angle; suddenly I was on my back, in the same position I would be during launch and reentry.

The capsule started to move, and I could feel the G-forces going through my chest, front to back, with so much force that it felt like multiple people were lying on top of my chest.

At first, it was hard to take a breath. I had been so worried that it was going to be painful. But it wasn't. It just felt like—like a really, really tight hug.

Then my vomit bag (which the team had included just in case I got sick) came loose and whipped past my face and flew around the capsule. And again. And again. There was nothing I could do to avoid it.

Then the world stopped moving. I stopped moving. The vomit bag stopped moving. I could breathe again. I hadn't vomited. My leg was still in one piece.

Before we left the facility, we stood together for a centrifuge graduation ceremony. We had completed our first training exercise!

"I'm looking forward to seeing you all fly," said the instructor. It was very sweet.

Just a short while before, I had been all nerves. Now I was riding high. A few weeks back, the others had been strangers. Now we really were a crew. I was part of a family, and the Inspiration4 team was much bigger than us four.

Kidd called me the day after our triumph in the centrifuge.

"Hey, Kidd!" I answered.

"Hey, G-Monster!" he replied.

I started laughing.

"We were watching you in the centrifuge," Kidd said. "You nailed it, G-Monster."

I smiled so big in that moment; I couldn't stop smiling. When they give you a nickname, it means you belong.

G-Monster 1, centrifuge 0.

CHAPTER 14

Upper Limits

SpaceX had designed a training program that would test us and prepare us for space in many ways. Jared, of course, wanted to take it up a notch.

Mount Rainier, in Washington State, is an active volcano more than fourteen thousand feet high. And we were going to climb it.

Jared wanted to us to learn to "get comfortable being uncomfortable." And what's more uncomfortable than climbing a mountain and camping in the snow?

The idea of this climb made me nervous. I love to be active, but usually I try not to take my leg into uncertain situations (you know, like centrifuges). In this case, I was worried for a few reasons. Cold weather tends to make my leg hurt. I didn't want to slip and fall in the snow. And I'd never attempted anything like climbing a mountain before and wasn't sure if I could even do it. But it wasn't meant to be easy. It was meant to serve as crew bonding, and I was always up for some of that. I knew that if I wanted to go to space, I couldn't pick and choose which training activities I wanted to do and which I did not. This was not a training buffet. I couldn't offer to get back in the centrifuge and skip the climb. If I wanted to be on this team, I needed to prove to Jared, Chris, and Sian—and to myself—that I could do it, training exercise by training exercise.

I have a gift for optimism, so I leaned into that.

I wasn't a gym person before I trained for space. After my cancer diagnosis, I hadn't been able to take PE classes, so aside from an occasional yoga class as an adult, exercise hadn't become part of my routine. I was told that stronger muscles would be helpful in the microgravity environment of space and for dealing with high G-forces during launch and reentry.

When I finally told my SpaceX doctor how little exercise I was getting, he connected me with a trainer. I was feeling motivated to get moving! In the first workout she sent me, I walked on the treadmill for twelve minutes and felt absolutely miserable.

She sent me workouts every day, motivated me, and

held me accountable. Soon I could lift heavier weights. I could go longer on the treadmill and exercise bike. I could even balance better on one leg.

"Your arms are looking really toned," one of my friends said, a few weeks into my new routine, and that was something I loved to hear.

I could feel myself getting stronger, and it felt incredible.

Every day, I increased my treadmill time and incline until I was walking for over an hour with the incline as high as I could get it. A few days before the climb up Mount Rainier, I hit seventy minutes on the treadmill with ease. I was so proud of how far I had come in that month of training.

I called Jared and said, "I hit seventy minutes on the treadmill. Do you think I'm ready for this?"

His "yes" in response didn't sound quite as confident as I had hoped.

Even though I was worried, I still felt the rush of optimism flowing through me.

Training in space happened in blocks of time. When I wasn't training, I was back at St. Jude working with my patients. It was an intense schedule.

One day, a patient and her mom stopped me in the hallway.

"Are you Hayley?" asked the mom. "The girl who's going to space?"

"Yes," I said. "That's me!"

I was used to people asking me about my space journey now, and I loved to share about it.

I started talking to them and learned that the little girl had been having a hard time.

"Last night I saw that my brothers and sisters were running and jumping around and I felt sad. Because of my cancer I can't run or jump like them."

"I can't run or jump like my little brother either because of the cancer I had," I said. "But it's not going to stop me from going to space."

She looked at me, processing this.

"You don't need to run or jump to do big things," I told her.

It was so special to be able to relate to her in that way. I don't know how big that moment was for her, but for me it was huge. She reminded me of why I was going to space in the first place. I was going to show these kids with cancer that they could still do big and wonderful things. Having cancer wasn't going to stop them from doing anything.

After a week at work, it was back to training: climbing Mount Rainier. The day before we started, we met our mountain guides at the camp near the start of the climb, and they ran through the plan and gave us a safety lesson. Then we showed them our gear. My new backpack was half my size.

Kidd showed me how to put spikes called cram-
pons onto my mountaineering shoes to keep me stable
as I walked in the snow, and he walked me through how
to use my new gear.

"Is your backpack too heavy?" he asked.

"No," I replied, though I wasn't sure how true that
was.

The small town outside of Seattle was blanketed in
fog. I couldn't even see the mountain we would be
climbing the next day.

We were staying at the main lodge in town for the
night. After unpacking and repacking my backpack, I
stretched out in the bed, enjoying every minute I had
left in the warmth, knowing we would be leaving early
for the climb.

Bliss.

Followed shortly by the buzz of my alarm at
6:00 A.M.

Early the next morning, sitting in the backseat of
the SUV, listening closely as Jared provided us with last-
minute tips for the climb, I thought, *I'm ready . . . to get
this over with*.

We gathered at the start of the trail with our guides,
Kidd, and our other mission director, Leif. Leif was
also a friend of Jared's, a former air force test pilot, and
an aerospace engineer. A film crew for our documentary was there to capture the glamour of the climb.

They positioned us in a single-file line, and I took

my place behind Sian. I asked Jared to walk behind me because I felt like he had the best potential to catch me if I fell. We grabbed our hiking poles and set off. Our guides instructed us to take one step at a time, leaning on the leg that was planted with each step and taking sharp exhales.

I watched my feet for the next nine and a half hours, cautiously taking step after step. My strategy was to step into the flattened snow where the person in front of me had already stepped, because it's sturdier. Still, there were moments where I would step forward, the snow beneath my foot would give way, and I would stumble. When we went up steep inclines, I sometimes had trouble reaching the next step. When we went downhill, I sometimes had trouble bending my leg enough to take a large step down.

My crew was constantly checking in on me.

"How's the leg holding up?"

"Fine," I would reply, or "Good."

I was not planning to say otherwise until I was really struggling.

Every forty-five to sixty minutes, we stopped for a break to reapply sunscreen, sip water, and eat snacks. Leif and I would share dark chocolate. I took selfies with my crew, the amount of ice frozen to my hair in the photos increasing at each stop.

I asked the guides for updates on how far we had already climbed, in percentages. Around the 65 percent mark, I started to feel woozy. Not just woozy. I saw dark stars creeping into the corners of my eyes. I knew what that meant.

I mentioned to the physician that I was feeling like I was getting close to fainting, just so she would be aware. My tone was as casual as possible. I felt like I could power through it, though, and I took large gulps of water.

I started reciting a new mantra to myself: *Can't faint, must go to space, can't faint, must go to space.*

The guides recommended that I work on making sharper exhales, since we were reaching higher and higher altitudes. After a few minutes of trying that, the stars went away and I felt stronger.

The whole way up was difficult for me. There wasn't one easy moment. I was very aware of the camera crew documenting every step. A few times when I had trouble taking a step up an especially steep incline, I felt the camera watching me struggle. I was a tad annoyed, because I was trying my very hardest and I didn't want to look weak on camera.

Thinking about my patients helped me through. We ask a lot of them, these kids going through cancer treatment, and they don't complain. What they're doing is a lot harder than just climbing up a mountain. The whole way up, I thought about how I was doing that mountain climb, and the whole mission to space, for them.

I also thought about my own cancer journey. My mom's mantra throughout my treatment was "One day at a time." We couldn't think about how many more cycles of chemo I had left to go, because if we did, it felt too overwhelming. We could concentrate only on that one day, that one moment. I couldn't think about how much longer I had left to climb to reach our destination. I had to concentrate on my one step, followed by one other step.

The other thing that sustained me was my dad's belief in me.

Just after Dad died, we were going through some old bins in our garage when I found the board he had signed when we got our brown belts: "I'm more proud of you for conquering your fear than for earning your brown belt." After I found that board years later, I put it in my closet so I could see it every day. My dad wouldn't have cared if I had made it up that mountain or not. He would have cared only that I'd tried. He would have wanted me to push through my fears so that I could do what I wanted to do.

With his voice in my ear, I kept going.

We were in the clouds throughout the climb, so we could never see more than a few yards ahead of us. This helped me stay in the moment.

Nine hours in, we were so close. At this point the

clouds were clearing and we could see Camp Muir, our goal, in the distance. Since our altitude was so high, each step felt heavier, and each breath was becoming more labored.

"Fifteen minutes and we're there," Jared encouraged us.

"We can do anything for fifteen minutes!" I replied.

The four of us changed formation. Now instead of being in a single file, we walked side by side the rest of the way up. A victory climb. We took our final steps into Camp Muir, where Kidd was already waiting to congratulate us. Jared pulled us into a group hug (very uncharacteristic) and told us how proud he was of all of us. He couldn't stop smiling.

"You were the only one talking when we hit the high altitudes," he told me. "You seemed to actually get stronger the longer we hiked."

The whole way up, I was looking forward to the dinner I'd brought with me. The guides had hot water for us, but we had been expected to pack our own food. Always a picky eater before this trip, I couldn't bear the thought of freeze-dried food, so I'd packed several ham-and-cheese sandwiches along with potato chips for the trip. Rookie mistake. My ham-and-cheese sandwiches were frozen solid, and all of the chips had gotten crushed in my backpack.

Our doctor shared her freeze-dried pasta with me,

and I discovered to my relief that I loved it. Everything tastes better after a long day of hiking.

We were each assigned a tent where we'd be sleeping for the next two nights. Thankfully, they had already been set up for us. It was such a relief to take off the giant mountaineering shoes and several layers of coats. Despite being in freezing temperatures and sleeping on the ground without a pillow, I slept deeply, curled up in my sleeping bag.

The next morning, the clouds had cleared. Sian had brought plenty of tea to share, and I drank it from a mug while looking out at the spectacular view: stunning mountain peaks all around us, blue and white as far as the eye could see.

After breakfast, we hiked to a nearby ice cave and took turns being lowered into it by our guides. We didn't have to do it but all wanted to; when else would I have the chance to be lowered into an ice cave?

Now that I was going to space, things that would have scared me in the past were put in a new light. *I can do ANYTHING.* The words echoed through me, offering the promise of so much more.

The next day, it was time to hike down the mountain. What goes up must come down—the beauty of gravity. We packed up and started our trek down. Soon I was way behind the pack. Fun fact about my leg: While other people usually find going down easier, it's much harder for me. The muscles it takes to balance going down stairs or going down mountains are much weaker in my leg. Jared and a guide stayed near me to catch me if I fell. Still, I could take only baby steps. One of the guides offered to put me on a sled for the rest of the way. At first, I declined, being stubborn, but after an hour or two of moving at a snail's pace, I took him up on the offer. Guides took each corner to control the sled as we went downward.

I glided past groups on their way up the mountain, waving to them and smiling. The hard part was over for us. When we got back down to the bottom, we had a celebratory cheer.

We had done it! We had climbed to the top and back again! I felt absolutely overjoyed. I hadn't known how long the hike would be before we set off, and I definitely did *not* know I would be hiking for nine and a half hours up a mountain. If I had known that ahead of time, I would not have even attempted it. Instead, I had crushed it.

In that moment I understood that I had been putting limits on myself that did not need to be there.

I arrived back in Memphis at 2:00 A.M. and fell into bed, exhausted. Just a few hours later, at 7:00 A.M., I was back at work.

That afternoon, I met with my boss's boss.

"How are you doing?" she asked me when I sat down in her office.

"Ummm, tired," I said, smiling at her. "I just spent the last three days on a mountain."

I had been struggling with balancing all the training and studying and media appearances on top of my job at St. Jude, so I had reached out and asked for some help.

"That's what I wanted to talk to you about," she said. "We want you to take a break from your PA job so that you can focus on your astronaut training."

I burst into tears. I knew they weren't firing me, but I loved my PA job and didn't want to take a break from it. Even a short break was too long.

"Your manager told me this was going to make you sad," she said, handing me a box of tissues.

"But this job is my purpose in life," I said.

Now I was really crying.

"This is exhibit A that I'm exhausted," I explained through my sobs. "I don't normally cry like this."

Stepping away from my patients felt like the ultimate sacrifice. It hurt, but I eventually stopped crying and agreed that I would take a temporary step away to focus on becoming an astronaut. Emphasis on "temporary."

I told myself that I'd still be very connected to St. Jude, and that I'd be able to talk to the kids from space. Besides, I knew I'd be back.

CHAPTER 15

Inside the Simulations

I threw myself full force into training, the majority of which was spent in the Dragon capsule simulator at the astronaut training center in California. At times, we'd be in the simulator for hours. We were either spending time getting to know the model of our living quarters or going through mission simulations with unexpected problems the trainers would throw our way. We were always prepping for whatever simulated emergency might come up next.

We wore our training space suits only when the situation demanded it. The rest of the time, we'd be hanging out in casual Inspiration4 gear and fun, colorful socks, since you don't need shoes in space. On the actual mission, we would be wearing our space suits for launch, for reentry, and if there were any emergency situations.

Midway through training, we practiced our first launch simulation, as if it were launch day. Mission control was present. So was the crew who would be loading us into the capsule on launch day.

Jared kept reminding us that we needed to take it seriously and focus. I felt strong and confident, ready for anything.

We were training in real time. At launch, we would be strapped into the capsule about two and a half hours before liftoff. We'd be using that time to go through launch procedures, but mostly waiting while the rocket booster was loaded with fuel. The ground crew would be working hard during that time to make sure we would launch safely.

Today part of what we would be practicing was the waiting. No sweat.

We sat there and sat there. And sat there. As we sat, my leg started to feel stiff. Because of the angle of the seat, it was forced into a bent position and I couldn't move it.

I took a deep breath and told myself it would pass.

Stiffness became pain. The pain became intense.

I looked around. Sitting there didn't seem to be bothering anyone else.

I started to feel a lot of pain. I kept telling myself that it would go away. But the aching grew worse. I could feel my face starting to grimace.

I was connected by radio with my crew. They were cracking jokes here and there, but I was silent.

Finally I said, "Y'all, don't say anything to SpaceX, but I'm in a lot of pain."

Jared, Chris, and Sian sounded worried: "Are you sure? Anything we can do?"

"Yeah, don't say anything."

I could feel my face really grimacing now, my eyebrows knit tight. The ache was so intense that I was sweating.

I took a breath and said, "Don't tell SpaceX, but I really am hurting."

Jared immediately called the ground crew. "Hey, we need to stop the simulation. One of our crew members is having trouble."

My commander knew what I needed, even when I had trouble asking for it. And then they shut it all down, they opened the doors, and a crowd of people came in yelling, "What's going on? What's going on?"

I hated the drama and the attention. I wished I hadn't said anything, I wished I could rewind time or just make everyone calm down. And so I said, "Everybody's being really dramatic."

Someone said, "Get the doctor."

The doctor, my friend Anil, came in.

"My leg's killing me," I told him. "I'm so sorry."

And I burst into tears. I cried and cried.

"My leg did *great* climbing Mount Rainier, and it's being taken out by sitting in a chair?" I said through my tears. I was so embarrassed that the simulation had to be paused on my account. I couldn't believe it. Painful feelings began to resurface—in that moment, I felt like the cancer girl once again, like I couldn't keep up.

I kept saying, "I'm still the toughest crew member!"

Anil said, "Look. No one's ever done this before with a prosthesis. You're the first one. This is new for us, and we've got to figure this out. We will fix this."

That made me feel hopeful.

He was right. We needed to figure out a seat that would work for me, and many more people to come. People with prosthetic body parts would one day be going to space after me. I was opening up space travel to people like me, who aren't physically perfect.

I had pain that entire day and into the next day, because I had waited too long to ask for help. Note to self: You should always speak up when you are in pain. You should never have to feel bad about the experience you're having in your body.

SpaceX took the problem very seriously. They had a "We've got to fix this" attitude. They held meetings the very next day to redesign my footrest, and they made a new seat for me where my leg was more extended so that I would have no pain on launch day.

The next challenge thrown our way was altitude chamber training. We flew to Durham, North Carolina, so that we could be exposed to two environments: high carbon dioxide and low oxygen.

Since everyone can have different symptoms when carbon dioxide and oxygen levels go up or down, the goal was for each of us to experience and understand our own reactions. This way, if there was a problem with our environment in space and the levels were off, we'd be able to realize it quickly. We started with a classroom lesson, learning all about hypercapnia (high carbon dioxide) and hypoxia (low oxygen).

Hypercapnia training required us only to breathe into a fancy tube that would basically recycle our own breath, increasing our carbon dioxide. I felt tingly and light-headed, which was followed by a killer headache.

For hypoxia training, we were placed in an ancient-looking chamber with creepy gas masks hanging from the ceiling. We had oxygen masks on while they reduced the oxygen in the chamber, and then, one at a time, we removed our masks. Since hypoxia can cause confusion, the instructors had a list of tasks for us so they could see how we were being affected.

Chris went first. He made some comments that had me questioning if it was regular goofy Chris or if it was the hypoxia talking.

Then it was my turn to take my mask off. I had an oxygen monitor on my finger to track my dropping oxygen levels. A timer was set for two minutes, and I had a list of tasks to complete. If my symptoms were severe, they would tag me out early.

I initially felt fine, then became more self-aware. I realized I was feeling the effects of the hypoxia.

I turned to Chris with a smile and said, "I feel *great*!" I felt incredibly silly, which, as it turns out, is not how people usually feel.

They asked me to count backward from one thousand and write the numbers on a piece of paper. I started fast because I wanted to see how far I could make it (and make it further than my crewmates).

As time went on and my oxygen levels continued to drop, my handwriting became sloppy. I made it to 900, then stopped in my tracks. What was one number less than 900? I couldn't think of it. I wrote 929, then scratched it out. Again I wrote 929 and scratched it out. I looked at Chris. Then it came to me: 899! I wrote out a few more and looked at my oxygen numbers on the monitor. It was 38 percent. For the record, normal is 95 to 100 percent.

Normally this would have really freaked me out, but I trusted the team running the training. A few seconds after I put my oxygen mask back on, I felt normal. I looked down at my worksheet and saw the increasingly messy handwriting and laughed.

No doubt, I'd be able to recognize that hypoxic feeling again.

Our reward for climbing inside all of these simulations: We went to Nevada to take a zero-gravity flight so we could experience microgravity before we got to space.

This special plane would fly in a way that would let

the passengers experience temporary microgravity. We got to experience twenty or thirty seconds of zero gravity sixteen different times.

Please note that this flight has historically been nicknamed the "vomit comet."

It was pure chaos. Bodies flying everywhere, running into one another, people scream-laughing. I got kicked in the face. A few times I wasn't sure which way was up or down. When gravity would suddenly come back, we would hit the deck pretty hard.

Navigating in microgravity is harder than astronauts make it look! As time in the zero-gravity flight went on, my movements became somewhat more controlled. I went into the zero-gravity flight thinking it would be pretty cool, but I had no idea how much fun I would have. I even did flips.

I could barely contain my excitement knowing I had three whole days of nonstop zero gravity coming up.

CHAPTER 16

Nova

I met the Dragon for the first time in July.

The crew and our SpaceX training team were down in Cape Canaveral for a few days of training, walking through what launch day would look like, as well as running through launchpad emergency situations.

And there it was, finally, our Dragon capsule. It had already been to space once, taking a crew of NASA astronauts to the International Space Station. It was so exciting to look at it and think, *That is our spacecraft. That will be our home in space for three days!*

Our Falcon 9 rocket booster was there too. The first stage of the rocket is reusable, and this would be its third mission. I had seen a few boosters before, and every time I did, I was amazed by their height. Ours was covered in soot from its previous space missions, and we signed our names in the soot. Of course, I then wiped the space dust on my trainer.

There was a lot of ground to cover, and one very important part of it was the food.

My friends would always ask me what I was going to eat in space. I told them I didn't really care; I could eat anything for three days if it meant I was in space. When I first tasted some of the food options they were offering us, I wasn't as sure.

On our spacecraft we couldn't heat food, and we couldn't rehydrate freeze-dried food, so on food-tasting day we were presented with a variety of shelf-stable options that wouldn't create crumbs. Crumbs could become dangerous in space because they could float through the air and get in someone's eyes or even affect hardware. For example, instead of bread, we were given tortillas as an option because they produced fewer crumbs.

I was optimistic when I saw the pile of different types of food in various wrappers and packaging, but after a few tries of shelf-stable pasta and meats, my smile faded.

Then there were the "food cubes," which the food engineer was very proud of. They were small, brightly colored cubes that were made of salmon, avocado, and kale, and we were the first crew he had presented them to. I gagged. The texture was like Jell-O but somehow also chalky. And the taste was . . . as you would imagine shelf-stable salmon mixed with kale would taste. "I don't think I'm going to eat much in space," I told Sian as I wiped my eyes. My crew shared my viewpoint.

Jared tried some colors of the cubes but refused to try the others. The food engineer was visibly offended.

"They're not that bad, guys! I ate these for lunch the other day."

"Where's the astronaut ice cream?" I asked, assuming we would have the freeze-dried dessert that every kid who's ever visited NASA has enjoyed. I was told in response that "astronaut ice cream" is not actually eaten in space, as it creates too many crumbs.

They really wanted us to like the second food tasting. The choices for this round were more like comfort foods. At the end of the day, I selected white pizza with bacon and jalapeños, bagels with cream cheese, bacon, shelf-stable cheese, salami sticks, almonds, tortillas, peanut butter, Skittles, and M&M's. Plenty of options for three days.

Even though I wasn't working as a PA at St. Jude, I was often back on campus. One of my big responsibilities as the St. Jude ambassador was to do media appearances to raise awareness and money for the hospital. I was very aware of how important this was. No matter what else was going on with my training, I always tried to show up for interviews with all of my energy and joy, because I felt very responsible for making sure we hit the $200 million fundraising goal.

In the months before I went to space, I did hundreds of interviews from the studio at St. Jude. One morning, my publicity team called to say they had forty-four interviews scheduled.

"Wow!" I said. "When?"

"Tomorrow," was the answer. I was to have forty-four interviews over the course of six hours.

At the end of that long day, I asked my publicity team how much money had been raised.

They told me. Even though they sounded happy, I felt disappointed because it wasn't as much as I had been hoping for. There was so much work to do, so many kids to support. Even with Jared's big donation, how were we going to get to $200 million?

No matter what happened, I was going to try my absolute hardest to make sure that we not only got there but surpassed our goal.

Our next training exercise was one I had been dreading: water survival training.

It was a hot late-July day in Cape Canaveral when we got into a training capsule wearing wet suits and motorcycle helmets, since we couldn't practice in the salt water in our space suits. The purpose of water survival training was to train for the unlikely situation where, in an emergency, we would have to get out of the capsule and into a life raft.

Our instructions were to learn the best way to jump from the capsule into the water to swim to the life raft.

Each task was more difficult than the one before.

For the final exercise, someone got on top of the capsule and rocked it back and forth so that it felt like we were being swayed by strong ocean waves as we jumped out of the capsule and entered the life raft. We eventually all swam to safety. We were rewarded with Popsicles, which melted all over us while we rested on the recovery ship.

Then it was back to SpaceX for a thirty-hour simulation, which meant thirty hours straight in a tight capsule with three other people. In space, our capsule would be a lot more spacious, because we'd be able to float up to the ceiling. But that wasn't possible on Earth.

From the moment it began, we were busy simulating launch and life in space.

One simulated situation involved a sick crew member, and as the medical officer, I got to simulate giving a shot.

We packed and stowed cargo, had our meals, performed research, did media calls, and slept.

Throughout the thirty hours, we were serious, especially as our trainers kept giving us problems that we had to work through, but we also had fun with it.

"Alien sighting," Jared reported to mission control.

I laughed so hard my abs were sore.

"We're so funny in space," I said. "I can't wait for the real thing."

We flew to Montana the next evening for fighter jet training.

Before the crew took our flights in the fighter jets, Jared gave us a briefing. The purpose of training in fighter jets was to allow us to hit high G-forces (even higher than centrifuge training), and it was going to be uncomfortable. We had to learn to ride it out.

"When we're launching," Jared told us, "we can't just pause it; we have to endure it."

I had my own briefing with Kidd, who was going to be my pilot. He was a former fighter pilot and Thunderbird, and I knew I was in good hands.

"I want to hit high Gs, I want to do rolls, and I want to fly the plane."

He asked me how many Gs I wanted to hit, and I said as many as possible.

Kidd nodded and said he'd see what he could do.

We took a quick class on ways to eject from the jet if there was an emergency situation. Ejecting did not sound fun.

I put on my G suit over my black flight suit. The G suit would be connected to the jet. Its purpose was to prevent loss of consciousness, which can sometimes happen from high Gs. When I was experiencing high Gs, the suit would squeeze my legs and abdomen to keep the blood flowing where it was supposed to.

To further prevent loss of consciousness, we also learned breathing techniques and how to squeeze our legs when we were hitting high Gs. I wore a helmet, gloves, earplugs, and a breathing mask.

No lie, I looked cool.

Kidd helped me into the backseat of the jet, which is not easy to climb into when you're five foot two. With ejection still on my mind, I asked him if he'd ever had to eject before.

"No, don't say that," Kidd replied.

"I'm just asking!"

We lined up on the runway and he asked me if I was ready to go.

"Let's do this," I said.

We took off and the jet glided into the air.

This isn't so bad, I thought.

We met up with the other jets, and then Kidd flew to an area where we had more space to have some fun.

"Ready to pull some Gs, G-Monster?"

"Born ready," I said.

He pulled back the stick and we went straight up, gravity intensifying against us.

My G suit wasn't working, so I tightened my legs and abdomen as hard as I could and breathed as I had been instructed.

"Eight Gs," Kidd called out.

YES!

We did barrel rolls so smooth I could hardly tell we were momentarily upside down, until I saw the horizon dance in front and all around me.

Kidd granted my wish and let me take control of the plane, and in my excitement, I yanked the stick. The nose of the plane jerked up in response, and I didn't have control for long.

We met up with the other jets and flew together into the sunset. The colors around and below us were vibrant. We glided in and out of the clouds, and I felt at peace.

Since I joined Inspiration4, I had been very aware of everyone's call signs. Call signs are the nicknames that are given to military pilots and astronauts, names that often arise from a joke (usually at the person's expense). Your call sign, once you get one, is with you for life. Kidd's call sign was Kidd, Leif's was Leif, Jared's was Rook.

Jared had warned us that we would all be getting call signs later on in training. Now it was time for our naming ceremony.

The crowd at our naming ceremony was made up of the extended Inspiration4 team, our families, and SpaceX employees. Each of us took our turn in the seat at the front of the room. Members of the crowd stood up and shared their ideas for call signs for us, along with a little speech about why that was the perfect name.

I watched and laughed as Chris became Hanks, like Tom Hanks, because Chris did a great job of acting like a sick crew member. Sian became Leo after Leonardo da Vinci, because she's an artist with many talents. When it was my turn, I was highly amused by all the options that were floating around. The contenders:

Chihuahua, because I'm small but ferocious
Miley, because my go-to karaoke song is
    "Wrecking Ball" by Miley Cyrus
Comet, as in Halley's comet

At the end, one of the extended Inspiration4 team members, call sign Slick, said I should be named Nova.

"We could call you something easy like Comet," he said, "but your light doesn't flash by every now and again like a comet. It shines even brighter. Like a supernova."

So now I'm Nova. A new name for a bright and unexpected future.

CHAPTER 17

Launch Week

Quarantining with my family and crew at a complex near Cape Canaveral during launch week reminded me of living in the sorority house and having all of my closest friends within reach at all times. I was sharing a condo with Sian. Mom and Hayden and Liz had their own condo. Kidd and Leif were there, and so were my SpaceX friends. I'd become so close with all of these people, and I loved being able to walk down the hall to see them at any time of the day. I had imagined being so nervous in the days leading up to launch, but it turned out to be a blast.

There was one thing holding me back from completely enjoying myself. It was the call with the St. Jude patients that we were supposed to have in space. We were getting close, and nobody was giving me the plan.

I was worried the St. Jude families wouldn't know about the call because they hadn't been told.

I reached out to my contact at St. Jude.

"I'm so sorry," she said. "We can't make a live call happen with all the patients."

I felt anger rush through my body. I knew how much it would mean to kids going through cancer treatment to see a survivor in space. That would have meant so much to me while I was fighting.

"I want the name of the person who said no to this call," I said. "How do they sleep at night, robbing kids with cancer of this experience?"

"I know how disappointed you must be," she said. She had no idea.

"Did you all forget I'm risking my life? And this is the *one* thing I asked for."

I knew I was being dramatic, but I was caught in the rush. This wasn't just a trip to space for me. It was a mission with a purpose, and the purpose was these kids.

"I'll make some calls," she said. "I'll see what we can do."

I spent the next few hours feeling upset and worried. I had already told some of my patients about calling them from space, and I didn't want to disappoint them. I wanted more than anything to bring them into that experience with me, because I felt it would be the most powerful way to show them that they could do this too.

A few hours later she called back and said they had a plan to make the call happen. "We had to get creative," she said. "We have a plan to use multiple video-conferencing programs at once, but we think it's going to work."

"Thank you," I said, grateful and gushing. "Thank you so much!"

With that taken care of, I could relax and enjoy the week.

I loved getting to know my crew's family and friends on a deeper level. The SpaceX family support team provided our meals and we all ate together, then hung out and played card games.

September 10, 2021, just days before liftoff, was my dad's fourth heavenly birthday. I decided that I would look online for a bananas Foster recipe. I always try to think of ways to honor Dad on these anniversaries, like going to his favorite restaurant or eating his favorite meal or buying an especially beautiful bouquet of flowers, which he loved. My dad didn't cook often, but when he did, he cooked amazingly, especially the steaks he made for us every Sunday. On special occasions he would make bananas Foster, a Louisiana specialty when it comes to dessert.

Dad had taught me his bananas Foster recipe years ago, and now I was kicking myself that I never wrote it down. Though the details were fuzzy, I found a recipe online that was close to Dad's. Ingredients were gathered: butter, brown sugar, and cinnamon. We fried bananas, scooped vanilla ice cream into bowls, and covered it all with the warm, delicious, sweet sauce. Then we passed bowls around to our entire quarantined crew.

The group toasted, "To Howard."

"It tastes just like Dad's," said Mom and Hayden, dragging their spoons through their last bites. It was the biggest compliment they could have given me.

I was experiencing what it felt like to heal through time, especially with the right support and having something really big to look forward to.

It was the first time I didn't cry on Dad's birthday.

The main factor behind when we would launch was the weather. A 3:00 A.M. launch had been a possibility. Then, a few days beforehand, it was decided that we would aim for 8:00 P.M. on September 15. Personally, I was much more excited about a sunset launch than about launching in the wee hours of the morning.

Once we arrived in space, a little after 8:00 P.M., we would need to be awake for about eight hours to get all our tasks done and settle into our orbital routine. Anil led us in sleep shifting. Each night, we stayed up later and later until we were awake until 5:00 A.M. each night and then slept until around 1:00 P.M. My family tried to stay up with me as late as possible each night but couldn't get anywhere close to dawn.

During the quiet hours of the late nights, my crewmates and I would do last-minute studying, together or by ourselves. One night, we headed to a bay for a midnight kayak trip. Another night, we went on a run around our launchpad. (Well, the boys ran. Sian and I played music and danced as we walked.)

As we neared launch day, one night at 3:00 A.M. we went to visit our spacecraft while it was still in the hangar. The team working on our Dragon capsule was still working day and night, finalizing last-minute details before rollout—the dramatic moment when the spacecraft would be transported from the hangar to the launchpad.

At this point the capsule was connected to the Falcon 9 booster and lying sideways. We walked up a ladder to a raised platform where we could closely examine the capsule, trying to stay out of the way of the people working.

"Can I touch it?" I asked.

"Um, okay, you can touch it with one finger."

So I did. The newly applied white paint felt thick and rough beneath my finger.

The next day, we gathered in a nearby field with our families to watch rollout. The hangar doors opened slowly. We saw our spacecraft emerging. We all screamed. Mom and Liz grabbed their phones to take pictures.

"That's my rocket!" I said. Even though we had had that close-up contact with the spacecraft, there was still a feeling of awe and mystery around it. Seeing it at a distance was almost more impressive.

I looked up at the sky above me, wondering what I would find there.

We got to have another view of the rocket the next day, this time from above because Jared had arranged for a group of fighter jets to fly over it. From my seat in the jet, I looked down at the rocket sitting on the launchpad. It was from this spot that I would be lifting off the planet. I was awed and stunned by it all.

Dress rehearsal was a chance for the crew, families, and operators to run through the whole day of launch, exactly as it would be on the actual day.

We started the day by eating a practice breakfast with our families, as we would on the big day. We walked out and waved to an imaginary crowd. Our families waved us off as we climbed into the Teslas that would transport us to the suit-up room.

I rolled down the window and saw my mom, Hayden, and Liz smiling at me.

"Goodbye!" they called out. "Have fun in space!"

They were smiling so big, but I knew this couldn't be easy for them. I felt so guilty for putting them through the stress of watching me launch into space. But I also knew they wouldn't have it any other way.

My vision blurred as my eyes welled with tears. I've never been good at goodbyes, apparently even fake goodbyes, and in three days I was going to tell them goodbye for real. There was a chance that it would be the last time I'd ever see them, these people I loved so much.

When I got back to the housing complex, I talked to my mom about why I had gotten so upset.

"I feel so guilty for putting y'all through all this stress," I said.

"You do not need to feel guilty," she assured me. "I feel good. I feel everyone praying for me. I know everything is going to go well."

The evening before launch, we were allowed to bring our families to the launchpad. I hugged my mom as I looked up at the rocket, still struck by how tall it was. I squeezed her tighter. We went up the tower and I showed them the crew access arm—the long hallway I would be walking down the next day to leave the planet. I looked at my phone. It was exactly 8:00 P.M.

"Twenty-four hours, guys. In twenty-four hours, I'm going to be launching into space."

Our last night on Earth.

The Inspiration4 team gathered to cook burgers on the grill outside at our housing complex. I sat next to Leif at one of the picnic tables for a few quiet moments.

A few nights before, I'd had a conversation with him.

"Do you think this is safe?" I had asked him one last time. Leif wasn't just our mission director, he was also an aerospace engineer with a great deal of experience.

"Yes," he said, and went on to explain that everything in life carries risk. You have to decide for yourself if the potential benefits outweigh the risk.

Now it was a clear night and the stars shone above us. I felt excited and at peace with what was to come.

"Look up," Leif said to me. "Tomorrow you're going to be looking down."

I knew I would remember this moment forever.

Toward the end of the night, I was able to spend some time with just my family. We played our favorite board game, Sequence, around the table in my mom's apartment. I appreciated that they didn't let me win even though I was leaving the planet the next day.

After a while they couldn't stay awake any longer and hugged me good night. Before I went to my room, my mom sang me a song that she made up, to the same tune as songs she would sing to me as a child.

As I was going to sleep, I thought about the letters.

The day before leaving for launch week in Cape Canaveral, I had been sitting at my kitchen table with a stack of stationery, trying to write letters to my family.

It was something we had been advised to do by former astronauts: write letters to our loved ones in case things didn't go well.

I couldn't bring myself to say goodbye just yet, so I began by writing celebratory letters for my family to read after launch.

"Mom, breathe! I made it to orbit!" I started writing to Mom. "I can't wait for our reunion hug. But please don't squeeze me too hard."

Once those letters were written, ready to be handed out while I was in orbit, I knew it was time to write the goodbye letters.

I took a deep breath and told my family how much I loved them. I told them that I didn't regret going on the mission, and that they shouldn't have any guilt about letting me go because they couldn't have changed my mind anyway. I asked them to keep sharing memories of me forever and to keep my spirit alive.

Those letters were waiting on my dresser back in Memphis, just in case.

I fell asleep thinking about those letters, hoping my family would never have to read them.

CHAPTER 18

Countdown to Launch

"I'm going to space today," I told my reflection in the mirror, wondering when I would start feeling nervous. You're supposed to be nervous about going to space.

Some of my SpaceX friends came into our condo dancing to Cardi B. I had joked to them weeks before that I wouldn't launch unless they did that, and I had been right to do so, because their performance was very motivating.

Anil took us each into a separate room for medical checkouts. My blood pressure was the highest I'd ever seen it.

"I don't *feel* nervous!" I told Anil.

He assured me high blood pressure before launching off the planet is not unexpected.

My hair was braided into two pigtails. I'd had multiple discussions with the space suit engineers months earlier, and we had agreed that this was the best way to manage my long, thick hair in a space suit.

When we met up with our families in the parking garage, Chris wasn't ready yet, so the rest of us played music loudly and danced in the parking lot. At 3:00 P.M. we had "breakfast." Sian had a smoothie, Jared had a cup of coffee, and Chris had a few bites of food. My plate was stacked high with steak, avocado toast, and a pastry.

"Any last advice?" I asked my rocket scientist brother.

"There are more clouds than you think," he responded.

We walked out of the hangar, and this time, the crowd waiting for us was real. I spotted my best friends in the crowd, screaming my name and wearing matching T-shirts with my name on them. My face lit up. I waved and blew them kisses and shouted that I loved them.

We were loaded into the Teslas, and my family came up to my window.

"I'm *so* excited for you, Hayley!" Hayden shouted, visibly thrilled.

"See you in three days!" Mom said.

There were no tears. We were feeling great.

My crew and I arrived at the suit-up room, where our space suits were waiting. It was getting real.

Maria, who had initially fitted me for my space suit,

was there, and I was so glad to see her. She helped me dive into my space suit and close the zippers. The energy in the suit-up room was high; loud music played, and Sian and I danced.

Before we left, Maria gave me a hug.

"Godspeed," she said.

The afternoon was warm and sunny, and the rocket sat tall on the pad. At the very top was our Dragon capsule.

Imagine three Legos clicked together. That's what it reminded me of. The top Lego is the Dragon spacecraft. The middle Lego is the second stage of the Falcon 9 rocket. The bottom Lego is the first stage, with its nine engines.

In just a few hours, we would be launching. I went over the process in my head. After a few minutes launching on the first stage, those nine engines would shut off and the first stage would be kicked away. Then the second-stage engine would ignite, bringing the Dragon spacecraft—and us in it—into orbit. Once we were in orbit, the second-stage engine would shut off and that stage of the rocket would be kicked away, leaving a single Lego, our spacecraft, in orbit.

I wanted to see it all, but our space suits kept us from looking up easily, so we had to hold on to one another and lean backward together to get the full view.

Spirits were high. We were ready.

———

At the launchpad, the rocket was sitting next to a large tower with an elevator that carried us up to the deck where the crew access arm was. Before we entered our spacecraft, we were able to use the old telephone that sits on the tower. It's the very same phone that has been used for decades by countless astronauts to make their final phone calls to say goodbye to their families before they head into the unknown. The phone has large buttons to accommodate space suit gloves.

My mom answered, putting me on speakerphone with Hayden and Liz.

"I'm calling you from the launchpad!"

"I'm so excited for you," she said. "And so proud of you."

"Bye, love y'all!" I said, and turned to face the rocket.

I was the first to climb into the capsule, and Anil was there to help strap me in.

"How's your leg feeling?" he asked.

"Good!" I assured him. This was 100 percent true. I wasn't taking any chances this time. The other three crew members climbed inside and got strapped in. We performed communication checks with the ground.

"Nova, how do you hear me?" I heard from mission control in Hawthorne, California.

"Loud and clear."

"Bye, have fun in space!" said the team closing the hatch.

I waved back at them, fanning the air with my large glove, and the team closed the hatch.

The interior of Dragon was all clean white, with four seats in the middle. I was in seat number one, at the far left of the capsule. Beneath our seats were three rows of additional cargo and some free space.

Dragon has two windows, slightly larger than airplane windows. There was a door, the side hatch, directly across from the seats. It was from this hatch that we had entered the spacecraft and from which we would exit in three or so days (in the Atlantic Ocean).

There was another hatch we were very much looking forward to using on our journey, the forward hatch above us. Through that hatch was the cupola, a large dome window, the largest window ever flown in space, the coolest window seat in the galaxy. It was brand-new and had been created for our mission. Soon, soon, we would be in there. But not until we had all adjusted to being in space. For now, that door would remain closed.

The walls of the capsule were made up of panels. Behind each panel there were cargo slots that stored multiple gray bags with all of the things we would need: clothing, toiletries, mementos, water bottles, food, medical supplies, research equipment. The plan was to spend three days in space. Since conditions needed to be just right in order for us to reenter Earth's atmosphere, we had enough food and supplies to hang out for five days if we had to. We had our shelf-stable food available, but we also brought a fancy version of an ice chest to space, lined with frozen pouches of coffee that served as the ice packs. Our food was kept in separate metal boxes, each labeled with our seat number, the day, and the meal.

There was an important method to all of the organization. We had to be very particular about putting everything back where it belonged, as well as being careful not to move too much weight around the capsule. We received plenty of lectures about how important this was. If the weight distribution was significantly off, it could have bad consequences during reentry.

Chris, in charge of cargo, needed to keep track of how much we had eaten and drunk, and from which compartments we had grabbed the water. As the medical officer, I would address any medical issues and be in contact with our SpaceX physician on the ground. I'd also be taking the lead with our live events in space.

Jared and Sian were highly trained as the commander and pilot. For the most part, our Dragon spacecraft would drive itself, but they would be monitoring it, commanding specific procedures, and they were trained to take control of the spacecraft if there were any malfunctions.

T minus 2.5 hours. Sian played *Star Wars* music from her iPad and we all laughed.

"I spy something white!" I said to my crewmates.

The whole interior of the capsule was white, so they were not interested in playing.

It felt like any other day in our capsule simulator at SpaceX, so I kept reminding myself that this time I was actually on top of a rocket.

I kept waiting for the nerves to hit, but all was calm.

Around my left thigh was a satchel, packed with things I might need for the first few hours in orbit, with an iPad on top that I was using to read through procedures one last time. Hidden in the satchel was also a stuffed dog that looked like the golden retriever therapy dogs at St. Jude. It wore a silver helmet and a white space suit that had four silver stars on the chest.

There is a tradition among astronauts that when you reach space, you toss out a zero-gravity indicator, usually a stuffed animal. As tradition goes, if it floats, you know you're in space. This would be my job when we reached orbit. Each mission has a different zero-gravity indicator, and it is a surprise. Spectators do not know what it will be until the crew throws it toward the camera in orbit.

T minus forty minutes. Launch mode. We put the visors of our space suits down, because from here on out, we could be propelled off the rocket at any minute.

Jared activated the launch escape system, which would remain active until we got to orbit. If the Falcon 9 rocket were to have a problem during fuel loading or launch itself and be at risk of exploding, the Dragon capsule would propel itself away from the rocket to safety through the launch escape system.

T minus five minutes. "Let's do this," I said.

T minus forty-five seconds. "Inspiration4 is go for launch," Jared said to mission control. "Punch it, SpaceX!"

T minus seven seconds. I could hear mission control counting down from ten. We knew there was a two- to three-second delay, so we would launch a few seconds before they hit zero.

Jared could see the real-time count on his screen and was giving us his own countdown.

"Get ready! We're doing this!" he called.

LAUNCH. I felt a large jolt. The increased G-forces came on quickly, but they were relatively easy to handle. From outside I could hear the fastest whooshing sound I'd ever heard.

"We are going FAST!" I yelled. I had a huge smile on my face. This was fun.

About a minute in, the rocket slowed its acceleration; we were entering max-Q, the part of the launch with the maximum pressure on the vehicle. This was the most dangerous part.

I could see Jared's screen from my seat to his left and watched the clock and the G meter. The vehicle started increasing in speed again.

"We made it through max-Q!" I said. We fist-bumped.

After another minute, the main engines cut off and we were thrown forward in our seats, hanging by our straps.

Main engine cutoff is an expected phase: The nine engines from the first stage of the Falcon 9 rocket shut off so the engine of the second stage can start.

We felt a jolt as the first stage of the rocket was kicked away.

The seconds felt long as we continued to hang there. We waited to feel the shift.

The second-stage engine had to ignite, it just *had* to.

The ignition pushed us back into our seats and we cheered and bumped fists. The second stage brought higher-intensity Gs.

"I can't believe we're LAUNCHING right now!" I yelled out. It was just so smooth. Second stage felt a little bumpier, but just a little. I couldn't believe how smooth it was.

A few more minutes on the second stage, and we were almost there.

―――

I hung in that moment, feeling a sense of safety, feeling Dad there with me.

Before launch, so many people had told me that I'd be closer to my dad than ever when I was in space. That isn't how I viewed it. I didn't need to travel to space to be close to Dad, because he was with me all the time.

He was with me now, and I felt him there, keeping me safe. It was such a beautiful moment, and I felt it so completely that my eyes filled with tears. The tears shot back like torpedoes into my hair because of the high G-forces.

All of a sudden, there was total silence, perfect stillness, and my straps began to float. I lifted my arms and relaxed them, and they remained in front of me, floating.

We were still restrained in our seats. Another jolt indicated the second stage of the Falcon 9 had been kicked away. Around us, Dragon was coming alive.

I pulled the golden retriever zero-gravity indicator out of my satchel and let it go. Leashed by a string, it floated in front of me.

You know what they say. When it floats, you know you're in space.

We were in orbit.

CHAPTER 19

Cold Pizza for Dinner (and Breakfast)

Through the window, all I could see was darkness. Then dawn broke through, and pastel blues, purples, and white swirled into my line of sight.

"Is that Earth?" It wasn't really a question. It was just so unbelievable that I had to say it out loud.

"Yes," said Jared.

"Wow."

But there were things to do aside from feeling awe and wonder. A time line had been uploaded to our iPads before launch, and Jared kept a close eye on our progress, calling out regular updates to keep us on schedule. We waited for the call to unbuckle.

I was the first to release myself from the restraints; I undid my seatbelt and allowed myself to rise. My body floated, weightless in the constant zero gravity.

This new sensation took some getting used to. At first, my helmet knocked all over the capsule. I went to open a cargo compartment, and as I pushed on it, I was pushed back in return. There is a law in physics that says, "For every action there is an equal and opposite reaction." In space, that means the harder you push something, the harder *you* are pushed back. I quickly learned how important it was to anchor myself, usually with my feet, before applying any force.

It was more than an hour before SpaceX said we could take off our space suits. Sian and I went first. (The boys always let us go first.)

We were using the buddy system to help each other out of the suits, which weigh around twenty-five pounds on Earth. I undid the zippers and freed my hands and legs. Then Jared grabbed my helmet and I wiggled myself out from the bottom.

My space suit stayed suspended in the air.

After we took off our space suits and the long-sleeved shirt and tights we wore underneath, I put on my space clothes. In our meetings with the engineer in charge of our in-orbit clothing, we had each chosen clothes that made us feel comfortable. I picked short-sleeved and long-sleeved T-shirts, as well as leggings and long socks and a sweatshirt. My space gear was sleek, black, and fitted, with our Inspiration4 logo on the sleeve of my top and my name embroidered on the front: Nova Arceneaux.

Two of my crewmates began complaining about

nausea, and I sprang into action. Nausea in space is actually pretty common. In an attempt to prevent this, we had worn antinausea medication patches beneath our space suits and had additional meds available in our satchels, but my crewmates needed more.

I was ready for my medical officer's hero moment.

After discussing with our doctor in mission control, we decided that I would give my crewmates shots of antinausea medication.

"Oooh, I never get to give shots!" I said, very excited, since PAs rarely give injections.

"Don't tell me that!" one crew member replied.

"I mean, I perform spinal taps. I've got this."

I anchored my feet and each crew member anchored themselves. Then I stabbed them and administered the medication. Both were nausea-free after the injections.

The mission was saved.

Within hours of our reaching orbit, an alarm went off, one of the big scary alarms, meaning that smoke was detected in the capsule. I rushed over to my seat to grab my bag, which was positioned next to it and contained a breathing mask. I knew this sound well from training. There were three tones of alarm based on the seriousness of the situation, and this one was the most serious.

Mission control called. They said that one of the

three smoke detectors had gone off, but there was no sign of an actual fire.

We sat in silence. I held my breathing mask bag tightly. A fire in orbit would be life-threatening and potentially devastating.

We had spent many hours in training practicing our fire response, which was the most challenging part of training. I thought through the steps now as I sat there. We would each put our breathing mask on and connect it to a place on our seat to receive fresh air. We would then put our fireproof space suits on and receive breathable air from the suits. Then we would have to do an emergency deorbit and come back to Earth, landing somewhere unplanned. We would possibly sit in the capsule for hours or days waiting for rescue. Or if the capsule was on fire, we would have to exit the capsule and swim to a life raft. Water survival training would come into play.

Mission control called back saying they believed it was a false alarm due to one of the fans, which they had turned off from the ground, and they believed the problem was now solved.

I hoped that we wouldn't hear another one of those alarms for the rest of our trip.

We had a few sets of research to complete while in space. The goal was to learn more about how microgravity affects the human body.

Astronauts who came before us had reported a space "fog," or not feeling as mentally sharp in space, so we used iPads to take tests that evaluated our memory and how alert we were. These tests were compared with ones that we took before space and after space.

We performed ultrasounds of our large blood vessels, eyes, and bladders to see their size and shape in microgravity. We swabbed several places on our bodies; the swabs would be compared with samples taken before and after the flight to see if the bacteria on our skin would change from being in this small space together. We did this activity together because it was time-consuming and had several steps.

"Armpits!" I would say, and we would all swab and then store the swabs.

"Nose!"

"Toes!"

The hardest part of this was the trash. Whenever we would open the trash bag to put more in, other bits of trash would try to float out. One annoying part of zero gravity.

We also gave saliva and blood samples. The blood and saliva samples we collected were later compared with samples we took before and after space.

Collecting a saliva sample without gravity was very challenging. When we spit into a tube on Earth, it would fall to the bottom, where it was supposed to go. But in space, the saliva rose away from the tube.

I spat directly into the tube, but the saliva floated out and onto Jared's seat.

"Oops . . . Sorry, Jared!"

We were very forgiving of one another in space.

All the data collected from our mission was going to be shared with researchers throughout the world. And through our mission they planned to collect millions of data points in total.

I felt really good about this. As Sian always says, "Solving for space solves for Earth."

Dinnertime!

I found my "seat 1, day 1 dinner." Inside the box were stacked slices of white-sauce pizza with bacon, peppers, and jalapeños. It tasted delicious! I didn't even mind that it was mildly soggy. I stuffed one piece in my mouth, then gave a slice to one of my crewmates and asked them to throw it to me so I could try catching it in my mouth.

Epic miss. It sailed right past me.

Jared had a pack of peanut M&M's.

"Hanks! Leo! Nova!" He called us each by name and then threw the candies in our direction. We kept missing.

Our first throws to one another were hard and fast, since we were used to throwing objects in gravity, but we soon learned that it didn't require as much effort in microgravity. When we missed, the candy ended up ping-ponging around the capsule. That physics law was coming into play again. The more force we used to throw those M&Ms, the harder the colorful chocolates bounced off the walls.

It took a moment for us to land on the perfect technique: the slow and steady throw. Even with the technique mastered, I still wasn't great at catching food. When we missed, we had to track down every piece of candy. If we didn't, it could affect our computers, or show back up, in a bad way, during reentry.

Sailing around the capsule chasing candy was so much fun. I *loved* not being bound by gravity. I started doing flips, and I couldn't stop. I curled up in a ball and pushed off, spinning multiple times in a row, until I ran into one of my crewmates or a wall. I was disoriented after spins because I couldn't feel which direction I was facing or where I was in the capsule.

Mission control could see us, and they laughed at me when they called.

I loved every minute of the freeing feeling of floating. I was in heaven. When I had first found out I was going to space, I had so many questions for Hayden. I asked about being upside down in zero gravity, and he cut me off, laughing.

"Hayley, there's no upside down in space."

"What? Of course there's an upside down."

I didn't quite understand the concept until I was in

space. It's true that in space, being upside down feels exactly the same as being right side up. Since it all felt the same, I thought, why not be upside down?

Bedtime! I was so tired. I brushed my teeth (swallowing the toothpaste, since there was no sink to spit into) and prepared myself for bed. We were sleeping in sleeping bags. Mine was hovering above my seat, and I put my seatbelt around it so I wouldn't float off in the night. There was no need for a pillow, since my head wouldn't be touching anything.

I was a little concerned about sleeping in space, since I don't always sleep well with people around me. I can never sleep on airplanes. But I was exhausted and I needed to rest. I tried to channel my sleeping habits from home. I turned on season 4, episode 1, of my favorite show, *Schitt's Creek,* put in my earpieces, and connected them to my iPad.

I slipped the fabric headband that held my bangs back forward over my eyes. I have slept with an eye mask every night since I was in the hospital at age ten. My grandmother gave me my first eye mask, hoping it would help me shut out the lights of the monitors and the nurses' station.

I fell asleep within seconds, and I slept more soundly than I usually did on Earth.

I woke up the next morning to find myself levitating, which felt oddly normal. I unbuckled and slipped out of the sleeping bag, pushed off my seat and up into the air, and did a few flips to greet the day. Then I propelled myself over to the coolers and dug out one of the coffee ice packs. That first morning in space, it was still mostly frozen, so I could take only a few sips. The second morning, it was the perfect temperature for a cold brew. That space coffee was just delicious.

I drank from the pouch and looked through the window at Earth, thinking, *Morning coffee with a view.*

My crew and I had been told we would get really close in space, and it was true.

When the SpaceX psychiatrist interviewed me before we started training, one of the questions she asked was "Do you get claustrophobic?"

I told her all about the time I spent in New Zealand in my twenties living in a camper van with three friends. True, I had never been in a camper van that orbits Earth at 17,500 miles an hour, but I was confident in my ability to have a great time in tight quarters, and I was right.

Before the flight, we had uploaded a playlist with each of our favorite songs on it, which meant that we had a great range of musical genres. One of my selections was "All Star" by Smash Mouth, in honor of my ten-year-old self dancing in the hospital and how far she had come.

We drank water from bottles that had a piece of Velcro attached so we could stick them to other pieces of Velcro around the capsule when we weren't actively drinking from them. I was less thirsty in space and had to remind myself to drink water. The bottles were often accidentally kicked, dislodging them from their Velcro attachments. We would float around the capsule tracking them down, quickly becoming familiar with the areas where items were most likely to float off to and get stuck.

We ate all of our meals together, laughing and taking pictures and videos, watching our food float in front of us. We didn't use plates, since the food would have floated right off them. Mealtimes could be tricky, what with trying to hold on to the metal container of food (while not letting the other bits of food float out) while also eating, drinking, and holding on to something to keep from floating away.

We shared and traded food like in grade school. Chris offered a Pop-Tart, which I took a few bites of. While I was chewing, he made me laugh, and with my "PAHAHA," the Pop-Tart crumbs shot out of my mouth and formed a cloud that hit Chris and Sian.

"I'm sorry," I said with my mouth full, causing more crumbs to spill out. They laughed as I tried to gather the crumbs floating in the air and put them back in my mouth.

For some reason I was the only person who ended up with bacon, so I shared it with everyone. My only request was they had to catch it in their mouths if they wanted it. We were still perfecting the slow throw, or maybe it was the slow catch that was the issue.

Even though it was fate and a lottery and a social media contest that brought us all together, I couldn't have asked for a better crew to go to space with. It felt like we were always destined to be the crew of Inspiration4.

CHAPTER 20

Around the World in Ninety Minutes

On day two in space, it was finally time to open the forward hatch and enter the cupola.

Chris grabbed the handle, turned the lever, and opened the hatch slowly. As he did, I got a glimpse of our bright, colorful Earth.

"WOW!" I said.

Still, I allowed myself to stare for only a few seconds while the hatch was being opened before shifting into work mode.

"All right, we've got some work to do," I said, and did the tasks I was assigned for the hatch-opening procedure.

Then I looked up and Earth caught my eye again. I could see the entire 360-degree view of Earth all at once. I could see the whole circle of the globe. I froze.

I was suspended, floating, paralyzed by the beauty in front of me.

Earth is so gigantic, yet so small I could see it all in one view. I finished my tasks and was the first one to float up into the cupola. Wide-eyed, I couldn't stop staring at Earth. It was the most beautiful thing I'd ever seen, alive, moving and shifting in front of us.

Around Earth, we could see the total blackness of space. I was struck by how 3-D Earth felt. I had seen so many pictures and videos of our planet throughout my life, but actually seeing it from that point of view, I was able to see the depth of the clouds and the expanse of the curvature. It felt real in a way I had never seen before.

The moon, nearly full during our mission, hung off to the side. Throughout our orbit, the moon danced around, showing up in different places from our perspective.

The bright, blue line of atmosphere circled the planet.

"It's so thin," someone said.

Hayden was right. Earth was all covered in clouds.

Former astronauts had spoken to us about the overview effect, when someone sees Earth from space and it changes them and their perspective forever. To be honest, I didn't experience the overview effect on the first day. But when I saw Earth from the cupola, and could see my entire home planet in front of me, something inside of me changed. I was so shocked by the beauty and the realness of seeing our planet. Earth was the most beautiful thing I had ever seen, and I felt a strong need to protect her.

How am I getting to experience this? I thought to myself. How was I so fortunate? When I went to space, fewer than seventy women had been to space, fewer than six hundred people total . . . in all of human existence. And I was one of them. The feeling of gratitude was overwhelming. I knew that feeling would stay with me forever.

We orbited Earth about every ninety minutes, so we spent about forty-five minutes in daylight and forty-five minutes in darkness. We moved quickly. Passing the United States took about eight minutes.

Passing over a sunrise or sunset revealed some of the most beautiful scenes. The first sign of sunrise was when the horizon would light up with bright-blue light. The land and sea and clouds below would at first come into focus in pale colors, but the colors would become more brilliant as the light spread overhead.

Sunset was especially beautiful, as the white clouds became mixed with vibrant purples, pinks, and oranges. The clouds would cast long shadows into the darkness that followed. There was a relatively sharp line of darkness, and it was nighttime.

The night passes showed bright city lights. A few times we even saw flashes of bright white lightning as a thunderstorm raged below us. During the night passes we could see stars, though I wasn't quite sure if any of them were planets.

Twice I saw a fast-moving and blinking object below. We suspected they were satellites. Sian, the expert geoscientist, and I saw a fuzzy, pale-green light just above the surface of Earth. She explained it was an aurora.

Based on our schedule, we were often awake when it was daylight over the Pacific region and nighttime over the United States. The oceans were vast, and although we spent the majority of our time over water, we joked that we were always over Australia. It felt like every time we looked out the window and I called out, "Where are we now?" a crew member would float over to our map and laugh.

"Australia again."

Australia was beautiful, a mix of deep reds and neutrals, and from our position we could see the entire continent at once. We even saw Australian wildfires from above, with smoke billowing toward us. I felt so intrigued as I studied the landmass. I had not yet been to Australia, and it made me want to go even more. Near Australia we could see New Zealand, and it brought back wonderful memories of trekking through the North and South Islands with my girls, feeling astounded at some of the most beautiful mountain views and fjords I'd ever seen.

I loved seeing the scattered, small South Pacific islands surrounded by bright turquoise waters.

"Oh, I'm moving these up on my bucket list," I said.

We passed over South America, over Chile and Argentina. The mountain ranges cast shadows on the land below, adding to the depth. I stretched my neck, looking for the rain forest farther north. More places I wanted to explore.

And as we passed over North Africa, I saw the brilliant red Sahara Desert, with its squiggly lines from windblown sand. I thought of camping in the Sahara right before the pandemic, sitting around a campfire with our Moroccan tour guides as they sang songs in tongues I didn't understand. There's so much to see and explore on our planet. I wanted to book a trip as soon as I got back from space.

Being in space changes you in physical ways as well as emotional ones. The SpaceX medical team had taught us all about the changes our bodies would experience in microgravity and how we would likely feel when we got to space. Each of us had slightly different symptoms while adjusting to microgravity.

A few hours after I got to space, I had a headache from fluid that normally is in my lower body shifting to my head in zero gravity. Jared described it as hanging upside down off your bed for hours. I had nasal congestion from the fluid shift, but I could still breathe through my nose, so I didn't take any medication for it.

We had been warned we would likely have back pain, because our spines had been exposed to gravity our entire lives, and suddenly being without gravity caused them to stretch. With the spinal stretching, I likely grew in space, but I didn't have a way to measure my height.

The back pain hit me the second day, and despite the warnings, I was surprised by its intensity. I curled up in a ball, tried to move in different ways to help the pain, and took ibuprofen around the clock. The back pain lasted for the rest of the mission, but it did start improving as time went on.

We all got a chance to connect with our families while we were up there.

They could see us on the live video stream from SpaceX, and we could hear them over the speakers in our cabin.

When it was my turn, my family shouted questions at me.

"How are you? How's space?" asked Hayden and Liz.

"How's your leg?" asked my mom, always concerned.

"I'm having the time of my life," I told them, talking into the cabin microphone.

I had been so happy to find that my leg didn't hurt at all. On Earth, after a long day, my leg was tired and sore. If I was in one position for too long—like that original space seat—or certain movements stressed the joint, my leg would hurt. In space, I had no pain— without gravity, there was no pressure or weight on my leg, even with all my spins and twirls. It was incredible.

"What have you been eating?" Hayden asked, which was an inside joke because every time we talked to my dad on the phone, he would ask what we were eating.

Then "SPIN! SPIN! SPIN!" they chanted, and I left the microphone suspended in the air as I showed off my zero-gravity spins.

I had a special moment with my dad too. I took his tie out and held it out in front of me. *Here you go, Dad,* I thought. Then I let it go. The colors swirled and whirled as the silky material unfolded itself and danced slowly in the air.

Zero gravity was a source of so much magic for me. When I first got to orbit, the top of my hair was still in braids from being in the space suit. I released the braids, then took off my cloth headband and released my bangs. My long, wavy hair floated around me in all directions. I whipped my head around and the hair followed and bounced. I was pretty obsessed with my zero-gravity hair.

My crewmates were very patient with my hair, even when it would hit them as I floated around. I didn't realize how much my hair shed until I was in zero gravity and every strand that I lost would wind up floating in the air. I noticed strands sticking to my crewmates' black clothing, and would try to pick them off without anyone noticing.

I knew the real reason I loved my wild hair so much. Losing all of my hair in cancer treatment was such a horrible experience for me. It was my first realization that I was truly sick. Ever since getting out of treatment, I've kept my hair very long, and I have been so proud of it. It's my symbol of health, of how far I've come.

I took a picture in the cupola with Earth behind me while holding a picture from when I was in treatment. In that photo, I'm bald, my blue eyes are shining, and I'm wearing a wide smile. I love that picture because even though I was in the height of my treatment, the height of being sick, I was still smiling. I think it's true of my attitude throughout treatment. And now here I was, in space with Earth as my background, holding that photo and showing the world how far I'd come. Smiling as big as ever.

I had packed very carefully to come to space, because I wanted this experience to be as meaningful as possible. I had thought about how to honor the friends I have lost to cancer. I've lost many friends whom I met at

St. Jude to cancer through the years, and I've never forgotten them and how much they mean to me. I've kept in touch with their families over the years, and I reached out to say that I wanted to bring their child's picture to space.

When we were in orbit, I took the photos out of the envelope in my bag. One by one, I went through them, seeing my friends' smiling faces. I spent a moment thinking about Luis, who had inspired me to study Spanish and follow my dreams. I missed each friend, but I also smiled, thinking about how good our time together was. Before I wrapped them carefully and put them away, I took pictures of their photos with Earth in the background, planning to send the pictures to their families when I got back to Earth.

I wanted them to know their children would never be forgotten.

The moment I had been waiting for ever since Jared first told me about our mission was finally here: our space-to-Earth video call with St. Jude.

"This is the most important thing we are doing in space," I told my crew.

My crewmates nodded, knowing how much this meant to me. We all had our own reasons for being here. This was mine.

Seeing how enthusiastic my crew was meant so much to me.

We positioned ourselves in front of the camera. I was upside down, because I thought it would be fun for the kids watching, and I wanted them to believe I was really in space.

"Hello, everyone, and welcome to our Dragon capsule here in space!" I said into the cabin microphone. "My name is Hayley Arceneaux, and some of y'all on the call may know me as your PA. I work at St. Jude; I have the best job ever; and like y'all, I was a St. Jude patient as a kid."

The questions were amazing.

"Are there cows on the moooon?" one kid asked.

"What was your training like?"

"What is life like without gravity?"

"Qué hacen para divertirse en el espacio?"

"Are there aliens in space?"

We each took turns answering their questions, and I used my Spanish to answer the question about what we do for fun in space.

Jared helped me with a zero-gravity demonstration by throwing a peanut M&M at me, and I actually caught it in my mouth. *Boom!* On camera. Documented forever.

I floated to the top of the capsule, showing off our view of Earth from the cupola.

And I told them all how I truly felt, that we were doing it all for them. "I wanted to tell you that I was a little girl going through cancer treatment just like a lot of you," I said. "And if I can do this, you can do this.

I'm so proud of each and every one of you. I can't wait to tell you the stories when we get back to Earth."

I wanted our mission to show these kids, and everyone following along, that they could dream big dreams. I wanted to show them that what may seem impossible is possible.

One thing I'm pretty sure is that St. Jude is now full of future astronauts, because they all want to see for themselves if there are actually aliens out there.

CHAPTER 21

Splashdown

Sian and I sat in the cupola, staring at our home planet. We were just hours from heading back to Earth.

"It was a real pleasure to go to space with you," Sian said.

We looked each other in the eye. "You too," I said. She was my sister for life.

I knew that for the whole rest of my life I would miss this feeling of looking at our globe from space, with the moon dancing alongside.

I wasn't sure if I was ready to go home, but I was looking forward to fresh food. This last day in space I hadn't even eaten. People usually are less hungry in space because food moves through the gut more slowly. Plus, I was getting tired of the pizza.

I was so ready for the fried chicken I knew was

waiting for me on Earth. I took a few last pictures and last glances, then floated down out of the cupola.

I didn't look back, because it was too hard. I hate goodbyes.

We put on our space suits and strapped into our seats. I already missed my favorite sensation in the world, floating in zero gravity. At this point my abs were sore from how many spins I'd done in those three days, but I didn't care. It was worth every sore moment.

Dragon performed a few burns to lower our altitude and, finally, to bring us home. Similar to launch, we strapped in two hours before splashdown because of this.

Jared and Chris started watching a space movie on their iPads. I watched on Jared's screen for a few minutes, but I was distracted.

"How about we list all the ways we could die during reentry," I said.

My crewmates looked at me.

Looking back, it was a very morbid thing to bring up, but at the time I thought it would help to mentally prepare myself.

I started off by listing a few potentially bad possibilities.

Jared added a few more.

I became quiet again. It felt like a lot of things could go wrong. During launch we had the safety net of the launch escape system, but during reentry we had no backup plan.

I watched the clock counting down to splashdown time, the number getting smaller and smaller. Then it was time.

We put the visors of our helmets down. Dragon's burns were musical in my ears. Then I heard a whooshing sound. For the first time in three days, I started feeling weight, and it felt ridiculously heavy.

"Zero point three Gs," Jared called out.

What? This is only one-third of Earth gravity? It felt like I had people lying on top of me.

"And we have to make it to four point five Gs?" I asked.

After three days of no gravity, just that small amount of gravity felt intense. G-forces continued building. I breathed in the way we had been trained and focused on keeping my lungs inflated. I reminded myself it would be over in less than ten minutes.

As we started entering the atmosphere, from the window I could see bright flashes of light that looked like lightning. Then flashes of red fire. The windows fogged from the plasma on the spacecraft, and we couldn't see anything else. Our capsule, and all of us inside, shook slightly as we made our way through the atmosphere.

I thought back to the morning when I was eleven and my mom woke me up to tell me the space shuttle *Columbia* had broken apart during reentry and all the astronauts on board had died. I'm not going to lie; in that moment, as we were going through reentry, I felt fear.

We were falling through the sky back to Earth. Our capsule was on fire at about 3,500 degrees Fahrenheit. We were in a communications blackout, unable to talk to mission control.

There was nothing I could do about it. I just had to trust that we would be okay.

Communication was restored with SpaceX and we were told to brace ourselves for the first set of parachutes, which were about to deploy. I put my arms over my chest.

BOOM! BOOM! BOOM!

We heard what sounded like explosions. And as the parachutes deployed, our capsule was lifted upward. It started shaking and swaying harder than ever.

Jared told us not to celebrate the first set of parachutes. We needed a healthy second set of parachutes to live.

We were told to brace again, then *BOOM!*

The force from the second set of parachutes opening was slightly less dramatic, but the whooshing was louder than ever.

"Four healthy mains," we heard from mission control.

"THANK GOD!" I shouted. I knew at this point we were going to be just fine.

We were in normal Earth gravity as the parachutes glided our capsule down, slowing its speed. It felt peaceful, and we heard what sounded like a summer breeze outside.

Jared called out how many meters we had until splashdown. We put our arms over our chests in brace position again at two hundred meters. He listed off the numbers: "One hundred. Fifty. Twenty-five. Twenty. Fifteen. Ten. Seven. Three. Zero. Umm, negative three. Negative five."

There was no doubting when we hit the water. *BOOM!* It was a more intense impact than we had expected, but it didn't hurt. A wave hit our capsule. We both heard it and felt it jostle us, but we couldn't see through the windows. Our capsule rocked in the water.

"On behalf of SpaceX, welcome back to planet Earth," said mission control, as we cheered and fist-bumped.

"Inspiration4 is mission complete," Jared called back.

We had done it. We were home.

Our capsule was lifted onto the recovery ship.

As the side hatch was opened, Anil entered the capsule. "Welcome home, earthlings!"

He evaluated each of us medically, assessing the strength of our legs.

"My legs feel really weak. Is this normal?" I asked.

He assured me it was.

I was the first to exit the capsule. Before I did, I stood, and a medical team stood around me. They asked if I felt light-headed. Cautiously I said no.

As I stood there, Kidd came into sight.

"Zero-G-Monster!" he shouted.

"Zero-G-Monster? YES!" I called back. I loved my new nickname.

The medical team helped me up, and I climbed out the side hatch. I smiled and waved to the camera crew that was waiting and gave them a thumbs-up. I then walked into the medical bay, feeling dizzy and weak. I lay on the stretcher.

"Where's the fried chicken?" I said.

It was waiting for us, cold but more delicious than I could have imagined. I ate lying down, crumbs covering my shirt while the nurse took my vital signs. Above us, the moon still danced around Earth, and I could see the stars, and I still didn't know which of them were planets.

After we were all evaluated, we were loaded into a helicopter. Our families were waiting for us at Cape Canaveral.

"OH MY GOODNESS!" my mom screamed when she saw me, squeezing me tight. I squeezed back even tighter.

I was home.

What Do *You* Dream About?

There was a time when I didn't think I'd get to turn twenty-one. Incredibly, I not only got to turn thirty, but by the time I did, I had spent 10,947 days on Earth and 3 days in space. What a wild ride.

So many of my dreams have come true. Getting to graduate from high school, to study medicine, to work at St. Jude; getting to travel, to have adventures, to say yes to things, to keep looking forward: Getting to live was my dream. Going to space was never my dream. My whole life has been my dream.

There are still times when I think to myself, *I can't believe I went to space.* I know how fortunate I am to have experienced something so few have seen or felt. It still amazes me to think that I spent time floating in zero gravity. That experience of weightlessness will be with me forever. That experience of seeing our planet from space, the way the moon moved around her in the blackness, will be with me forever.

So will the feeling I had the evening we got back from space and found out that we had surpassed our $200 million fundraising goal for St. Jude. I was over-joyed. I had been able to take the anger I feel toward cancer—for taking my father and so many of my friends—and do something about it. All that hard work—the hundreds of interviews I did to raise aware-ness about our mission, the challenge of studying and training for space, the discomfort and fear that I faced at times—all of it was worth it. It truly felt like not only mission complete, but mission accomplished.

It was also incredible to learn that despite my wor-ries about the call with St. Jude in orbit, in the end we spoke live with fifteen hundred families on that call. When I heard, I couldn't stop smiling. Two decades after we first walked into St. Jude and Ms. Penny said that we were part of the family, it is still true.

A few days after we returned to Earth, we had a welcome-home party. Ms. Penny was there, with her kind eyes and sweet voice. She told me how proud she was of me, and I thought about how much she had meant to a scared ten-year-old and her mom all those years ago.

My cancer besties, Hannah and Katie, were at the welcome-home party, still healthy and cancer free, living their best lives. Hannah came with her fiancé and Katie was with her husband and two kids. Dr. Doom wasn't at my return party, but he was at launch, and I found out later that he had brought the model of my prosthesis to show Anil, he was so proud. (I have a photo of the two of them, holding the prosthesis up in the air.)

So many people I've known and loved through the years, who have been with me on the toughest days, showed up to celebrate with me on this happiest day. All my best friends and their families were there, and some of my favorite co-workers from the emergency department and St. Jude. Lizzie was there too, watching alongside my family. And a person who was recently added to the mix, Mom's new boyfriend, was by her side.

The day after I got back to Memphis, St. Jude threw a parade in my honor. I was loaded onto the back of Dr. Doom's convertible, with his wife at the wheel. The first stop on the parade was in front of the main hospital. Patients and their families filled the sidewalks, holding pom-poms and homemade posters. The St. Jude CEO had the microphone. He asked if I could have imagined when I first walked through the doors of St. Jude when I was ten that I would one day be welcomed back as an astronaut with a parade.

In moments like these, life feels like it's come full circle. The dreams I had don't even compare to the glorious, beautiful life I have been given.

I walked back into my job at St. Jude on January 7, 2022, just about one year after I first got the call to go to space. I was a little bit nervous and a whole lot excited to be getting back to my dream job. My very first patient of the day, a little boy with big, curious eyes, told me he wanted to be an astronaut. I was more than happy to share videos on my phone of what space is really like.

My space suit has been donated to St. Jude, and if he wants to visit it, he can. So can all the children, some on their very first day at the hospital, as scared as I was twenty years ago. I hope it serves as a symbol of what they can do too, how wonderful life after cancer can be. I'm the first pediatric cancer survivor to go to space, but as I tell my patients, I'm definitely not the last.

One of my first questions when I found out I was going to space was "Are we going to the moon?" I knew basically nothing about space then, and I am amazed how much I learned over the months that followed, all the way to becoming an astronaut. A few months after our mission, I was writing an email. I casually typed the phrase "the time I went to space," then laughed out loud. It's still so unbelievable to me.

Going forward, I plan to continue doing what I love the most: traveling the world. Space was an unbelievable experience, and it made me appreciate Earth in a new way, so much so that I wanted to get back down to continue exploring on the ground. There's so much to enjoy on our planet, so much beauty to see and so many people to meet and so many things to learn. I've got a long bucket list, and I think that's how it should be. I'll never stop daydreaming about my next adventure and having something on the books to look forward to. Plus, I owe it to Australia to check it out.

Since my return, I've been asked several times if I would tell my younger self, when I was going through cancer treatment, that she would one day become an astronaut. The truth is, I would not tell ten-year-old me that she would go to space one day. The beauty of life is that you don't know what's going to happen. Not knowing what will happen is why, even on your most difficult days, you have to hold on to hope that there will be better days, so great that you can't even imagine.

Not everyone has childhood cancer to overcome, but everyone has something. Everyone has something that hurts your heart, makes you nervous about what the future will hold, and even makes you lose hope. What I've learned in my life is to not give in to that sadness and fear, not to lose hope, no matter what. Happiness and hope are, at the end of the day, choices. And they are worth choosing.

People also keep asking if I've changed. Absolutely, yes, I have. I haven't changed into a different person. I've just become more me. I've seen my confidence and strength grow. I have pushed past the limits I thought I had and learned more about myself in the process.

Going forward, I'll know that the experiences I fear the most can be the most rewarding, and that true toughness means taking uncertain steps exactly as you are.

Now I see that you have to say yes to opportunities that can change your life, even opportunities that scare you. I see that following your dreams can take you to dreams you didn't know you had.

If you take the chance, you will feel, and learn, and grow, and become even more you.

Aren't you excited to see what comes next?

Acknowledgments

I hope this book shows that I am who I am because of the people who have supported me, lifted me up, and made me laugh through it all. I am beyond grateful to have so much love in my life.

Some particular shout-outs as follows:

Thank you.

To Sandra Bark, for helping make my dream of this book a reality, for understanding who I am and helping me share it with the world. You are the type B to my type A, and early mornings to my late nights, and together we made the perfect team.

To Eliza, Cait, Keren, and the entire team at Convergent, for believing in my story, for your wisdom, and for guiding me through this process.

To Mom, for cleaning up more vomit than anyone ever should, for being our family's rock, and for being the best friend, travel buddy, and role model. Thank you for always supporting my adventures, even when they make you scared. Because of you, I am me.

To Dad, for teaching me the importance of exploring the world and forming relationships with people along the way. I will always try to live my life in a way that honors your legacy and the deep love you showed our family.

To Hayden and Liz, for answering my innumerable rocket science questions and for always showing up. Hayden, you've been there through it all, and you are my go-to now and forever. Liz, I am so grateful for your loving support through Dad's sickness and launch week and everything in between.

To Aunt Kerryn and Lauren, my extended immediate family. I can't imagine going through life without the two of you.

To my girls, you know who you are. I became who I am with you all by my side. Thanks for being the best, most ride-or-die, supportive krewe a girl could have.

To my care team at St. Jude, especially Lizzie, Dr. Neel (Doom), and Dr. Jane. So many people worked together to help me not only survive but have an unbelievably positive experience with cancer that made me want to grow up and do what you do. Thank you for carrying me through the hardest days and helping maintain my spirit.

To Jared Isaacman, I'll never be able to express my gratitude for your trust in me, for bringing me to the stars, and for your friendship—as well as for your passion and commitment to ending childhood cancer. You're making the world a better place.

To the rest of my crew, Sian and Chris. The four of us will share such a special, unique bond forever. I couldn't have asked for a better crew. Also . . . thank you for your patience with my zero-gravity hair.

To the entire Inspiration4 team, who became family. We wouldn't have gotten to where we were without your tireless efforts, which were both seen and deeply appreciated. I love you all.

To the SpaceX team, who instilled confidence, kept us safe, and helped give us the most incredible experience.

To the ALSAC/St. Jude team, who believed in me and helped give me the opportunity of a lifetime.

And lastly, to my patients and their families, for being my daily inspiration. Working with you all is the greatest honor of my life.

About the Author

HAYLEY ARCENEAUX is a physician assistant at St. Jude Children's Research Hospital, a career she committed to at age ten, after surviving pediatric bone cancer at St. Jude. She served as an ambassador for the hospital when she joined the first all-civilian orbital space mission, Inspiration4, in September 2021, and spent three days in orbit. At age twenty-nine, she became the youngest American in space, the first pediatric cancer survivor in space, and the first astronaut with a prosthetic body part. She hails from Louisiana but is now living in Memphis, Tennessee, with her Aussiedoodle, Scarlett. She continues traveling and exploring the beautiful planet she gained a unique perspective on from space.

Twitter: @ArceneauxHayley
Instagram: @hayleyarc

About the Type

This book was set in Garamond, a typeface originally designed by the Parisian type cutter Claude Garamond (c. 1500–61). This version of Garamond was modeled on a 1592 specimen sheet from the Egenolff-Berner foundry, which was produced from types assumed to have been brought to Frankfurt by the punch cutter Jacques Sabon (c. 1535–80).

Claude Garamond's distinguished romans and italics first appeared in *Opera Ciceronis* in 1543–44. The Garamond types are clear, open, and elegant.